GW01018438

KIDS
&Co

Winning business
tactics for every family

ROS JAY

Editor **RICHARD CRAZE**

Published by White Ladder Press Ltd
Great Ambrook, Near Ipplepen, Devon TQ12 5UL
01803 813343
www.whiteladderpress.com

First published in Great Britain in 2003

ISBN 0 9543914 0 3

British Library Cataloguing in Publication Data.
A catalogue record for this book is available from the British Library.

Designed and typeset by Julie Martin Ltd
Printed and bound by TJ International Ltd, Padstow, Cornwall
Cover photo by Judy Hedger

For Jack, Ned and Hal

Contents

Introduction

Most of us spend several years working before becoming parents, and the majority of us continue to work once we have children. At work, we learn all sorts of useful skills – managing, selling, negotiating and so on – which we can apply in any organisation we work for. But when we become parents, all those hard-learned skills are useless. Or are they?

This book explains how our business skills don't have to go out of the window when we walk in through the front door. We may sometimes feel that the kids get the better of us every time, but here is one weapon we have that they don't: all those business skills we are familiar with and they know nothing about. Closing the sale, win/win negotiating, motivational skills, and all the rest of them. All we need to do is learn how to apply them to our children as well as to our customers and our staff.

Obviously there is no perfect way to handle our children so that we don't hear a single whinge or tantrum (more's the pity), but there are certainly techniques which make life a whole lot easier. These techniques may not always work at 3 o'clock in the morning, or when a favourite toy has just disappeared down the waste disposal, but they certainly work most of the time to make the atmosphere more pleasant.

What's more, as we know from our business experience, these techniques work on grown-ups. So they are effective with children right through those teenage years even when, like customers and staff, they have got wise to the techniques and know what you're up to.

As with any new parenting practices, you'll find that some of these techniques take a little while to establish. Many will go unnoticed by your children – although you'll notice the benefits – but some will be spotted instantly as a change of system. For example, the very first technique in the book: don't drop everything for your kids on demand, but let them know you'll deal with them in a moment. They may resist this kind of change for a while (alright, they *will* resist it until they've tried it), but once they know you're sticking to it consistently they'll give in to it. After they've given it a fair trial, they'll even realise that it benefits them as well as you. So stick with your new approach, and it won't be long before it pays dividends.

Business skills transfer amazingly well to parenting. You can get real value from techniques from customer relations through to teamwork skills, as you'll see. And what's more, once your kids have finally worked out what you're up to and learnt all your skills from you, you'll have done your parental duty and taught them enough skills to set them on a fast-track business career.

So don't worry about your ability as a parent. Follow these guidelines and you'll soon find that you deserve to be as confident in your skills at home as you are at work.

Customer relations skills: make your children feel they matter

Applying customer relations skills to your children means treating them as you would a customer. You might initially find this whole idea somewhat galling. After all, you're supposed to treat customers with deference, and give them whatever they want – hardly a technique that most of us want to apply to our children. And anyway, how can children be like customers when we all know that the customer is always right?

But look at it another way. We treat customers with as much friendliness and co-operation as we can because it works. Sorry to be cynical, but customers like us better and buy from us more often if we treat them well. Sure, the people who really understand customers well do it genuinely and with the best of motives, but there's no denying that it gets the response we want. Well, if it works on grown-ups, why shouldn't it work on kids too?

Actually, we know it works on kids. Or if we don't know it, we should. The Disney Corporation knows it. McDonalds knows it. There are plenty of businesses out there who regularly deal with kids as customers, and they can vouch for the fact that kids respond in just the same way as adults to the treatment they receive (although the adults usually take it slightly better when they're told that the product they really want to buy won't be in stock until next week).

So here are the core rules of good customer care, all of which will help you get the response you want out of your children. You should be familiar with all of them, so applying them to the kids – once you've got used to the idea – really isn't difficult.

Acknowledge the customer immediately

The technique: The idea here is that even if you're busy on the phone or with another customer, you should always let a newly arrived customer know that you've seen them. You should always be able to find time to say "I'll be with you in a moment", or "Sorry to keep you waiting", or at least make eye contact and give a polite nod to let them know that you'll deal with them as soon as you can.

Children are even worse attention-seekers than customers. A customer likes to feel that they are the most important person to you right now; a child demands to know that they are. So when your child explodes into the room where you're entertaining friends, or starts asking where their clean T-shirt is while you're trying to change the rear brakes on your car and order a take-away pizza at the same time, try this technique on them.

Children are a nightmare for interrupting, and every time they do it you're torn between two options, neither of which appeals. One option is to ignore them, in which case you can guarantee that they'll just get worse (as in louder, more insistent, more threatening and generally more unpleasant). The alternative is to drop everything for them. This has great short term appeal – that is to say, it works. But at the back of your mind there's that nagging feeling that you're not being a good parent. You're teaching them to expect people to drop everything for them (obviously).

This technique gives you a middle way. You neither ignore them *nor* drop everything. You teach them that they can have your attention if they will simply wait a moment. What's more, they will get your full attention, instead of the rushed, stressed, "Oh, what is it now?" response which they would get if you dealt with them instantly. So when they burst in on you with demands or questions, try saying: "Hi! I'm just putting out this small fire that Amy started, but I'll get you a drink in just a minute." As with a customer, keep the note of (understandable) irritation out of your voice if you possibly can. Using this technique, everyone benefits:

- You get to finish what you're doing first
- They may have to wait a moment, but the pay-off is your undivided attention when they do get it
- Everyone can stay in a pleasant mood
- You can give up the guilt, comforted by the thought that you are bringing them up to be nicer, less selfish and egocentric people

Greet the customer with a smile

The technique: Always get off on the right foot with customers. A smile sets the tone for a friendly and helpful exchange. Even if you can see a customer bearing down on you looking furious, with a product they bought from you only yesterday in several pieces under their arm… smile. It may not solve everything, but it will solve a lot more than *not* smiling will.

Children are always ready to meet a challenge. The second you raise your voice, or sound irritated, they are right there mirroring you in response. To a child, the best form of defence is attack. The only effective way to handle this characteristic is to beat them at their own game. Give them something positive to mirror. Let them see that they don't need to employ *any* form of defence because they're not under threat. If your opening gambit is a welcoming smile, it doesn't half take the wind out of their sails.

If you have any experience with customers, it is no doubt instinctive for you to smile whenever you greet them. And yet when we get home to the kids, the instinct seems to vanish. Of course there are times when it's natural to greet our children with a great welcoming smile and a hug and a kiss. But how many of us can honestly say that we do it *every* time?

If you can smile at an angry customer who you can see is about to make a complaint, then you can learn to wake with a smile as you say "Hello darling, lovely to see you. Gosh, you're not often up at 5 o'clock in the morning, are you?" Simply learn to retain your instinct to greet the customer with a smile, and bring it home with you. See your child as a customer every time you greet them, and they'll soon forget to go on the defensive at all.

Look at the situation from the customer's viewpoint

Technique: Never mind that you're due to close in two minutes and this customer wants to launch into a lengthy cross-examination about how exactly the camera they're buying works, and what each of these little buttons on the side does. Look at it from their point of view. They want to take photographs at the wedding they're going to tomorrow and they're not good at reading instructions – so obviously they need you to explain the thing to them now.

You and your customer have totally different agendas. You

want to get the place closed and locked up so you can do the paperwork and then get home and put your feet up. The customer, on the other hand, wants to buy a good camera and then learn how to use it before tomorrow's wedding. You know it's the customer's agenda that counts… simply because they're the customer. So you see it from their viewpoint and you patiently explain (three times over) how the camera works.

You see it from their viewpoint because you have to. They're the customer and it's your job to look at things from their perspective. But what about the children? Do you always see things from their point of view? Suppose you are in a rush to get to the shops and back in time to prepare dinner before your guests arrive. Your child, on the other hand, is refusing to get into the car until their favourite TV programme has finished in 20 minutes.

What usually happens in this situation is a blazing row. You get increasingly insistent that they get into the car NOW, they dig their heels in ever further, and before you know it you're not enjoying yourself at all. But nine times out of 10, if you look at it from your child's perspective rather than your own, you'll at least be able to compromise.

Imagine the tables were turned. You've been waiting all week to find out what happens in this episode of your favourite programme and, just as you're getting into it, your child turns up and starts nagging you to come outside and play with them. You wouldn't be too pleased, would you?

You'll find that looking at the situation from your child's viewpoint makes it easier for you to cope. Instead of feeling irritated, you feel sympathetic. Of course, they've still got to get in the car and come shopping, but at least you'll be more tolerant in the way you put it to them. Otherwise, from their perspective, not only are you trying to stop them watching their favourite programme, but you're giving them a hard time as well – insult to injury.

With this approach you're more likely to start out by saying "I'm sorry, sweetheart, but we've got to go shopping...". Altogether a less confrontational attitude. This gives you scope to look for a compromise, too, which you'll feel more inclined to do if you're sympathetic from the start. "How about we put a tape in and you can watch it when you get back?" Or: "Why don't we buy some of your favourite ice cream, to make up for missing your favourite programme?" (Obviously it was never their favourite programme before; it just suddenly became their very, very favourite when you told them they were going to have to miss it. But if you're magnanimous, you'll overlook that.)

To be honest, the most difficult part of this technique can be working out what your child's viewpoint actually is. The older they get the easier it becomes – broadly speaking – but the depths of a child's mind can be hard to fathom. Nevertheless, if you're two, it really is the end of the world if your toy car refuses to fit down the plughole.

Once they are old enough to communicate (roughly after the age of two but before the age of 13) you can, of course, ask them to explain their point of view. Simply say, "I don't understand the problem. Can you explain it to me?" Try not to sigh as you speak, but to adopt a tone of genuine interest and concern – just as you do with a customer whose needs happen to conflict with your own.

Once you get used to seeing things from your child's perspective it gets easier and easier – just as it did when you first learnt to look at things from the customer's viewpoint. You'll find that you start off with a sympathetic attitude, which keeps the atmosphere pleasant and makes compromise – on both sides – less painful.

And what's even more important your kids – like your customers – will feel that they are important to you and their feelings matter.

Find the need behind the request

The technique: Customers often fail to explain fully what they need, which can make it hard for you to help them. So you have to find ways to get them to reveal what they really want. If a customer simply says "I need a hat," it's impossible to know which of your 240 styles of hat they will want. But if you find out *why* they need a hat – to wear to a garden party, to keep the sun off, to keep their hair dry in the rain – you can narrow down the possibilities until you can give them what they need. You do this by probing and asking open questions until you have all the information you need.

Customers have nothing on children when it comes to concealing their intentions. For a start, customers are generally keeping back information because it hasn't occurred to them that it will help, rather than because they really don't want you to know it. Children, on the other hand, may have all sorts of deliberate motives for keeping you in the dark. Nevertheless, the techniques which work on customers also work on children when it comes to getting to the bottom of a request.

Older children may well try to keep quiet about their end purpose in case you disapprove. For example, a simple, "Can I stay at home this afternoon, instead of coming out with you?" may actually mean "Can I stay at home this afternoon because if you're not going to be here I can invite all my mates round to watch the unlabelled video Paul found hidden under his parents' bed?" Some judicious probing and questioning here may save you being lynched by a large group of angry parents who don't like what their children get up to in your house.

Younger children, on the other hand, often asssume you understand what they want when in fact you haven't a clue. And yet often you could perfectly well fulfil their request if only you understood the problem. For example, when your three year old asks you for a sharp knife, it's quite likely that you'll say 'no'. But if you delve deeper, you may discover that they want the knife in order to cut themsleves a slice of bread because they're hungry. Once you've identified this root problem, you can offer to make them a sandwich yourself. If further questioning reveals that they want to help, give them a blunt knife so they can spread the butter and the filling themselves.

The key to finding the need behind the request is to ask open questions. These are questions which require a full answer rather than a simple 'yes' or 'no' or some other one word answer. Open questions often start with one of the words:

- How (as in "How would having a video recorder in your bedroom be different from sharing the family video recorder downstairs?")
- What ("What are you going to do with the sharp knife if I give it to you?")
- Why ("Why do you want to stay at home this afternoon?")

Just as with customers, you need to ask about the *reason* for the request, not the request itself. If a customer asks for a hat, don't ask "What sort of hat?" You'll end up playing 20 questions:

- What colour hat?
- What sort of material?
- With or without a brim?
- What kind of brim?

- With or without ribbons and decoration?
- What price range?

...and so on.

If, on the other hand, you ask them *why* they want a hat you can narrow down the choice much faster. If they want it to keep the rain off, you've narrowed it down to a fraction of your range straight away. So you should always probe the reason behind the request, not the details of the request itself.

You may still have to ask a series of open questions before you finally get to the bottom of the matter. But concentrate on the hidden agenda and probe it directly. If you ask your 12 year old what they're going to do at home all afternoon, they may well simply cover up the truth "Oh, just watch a video." But if you probe the reasons – "Why this afternoon, when we're out? Why not come with us and watch it when we get back?" – you make it much harder for them to avoid giving you the information you need.

When it comes to small children, it must be said that there's a certain satisfaction in turning the tables and asking them a series of questions beginning "Why...?" But more than that, it may be the only way you'll ever establish the strange truth of the matter: "Oh, I see... you need a hat to put on your head so you can chase the cat under the table and it won't hurt if you bang your head. Of course, silly me."

Behave as you would have the customer behave

The technique: This rule of customer care is all about the fact that people respond to us in the same mode in which we communicate with them. So if we are always open, friendly and positive towards customers, our customers will be open and friendly in response. If, on the other hand, we are unfriendly and unhelpful towards our customers, they will be unfriendly and difficult back. This is why some people seem always to attract easy, friendly customers while others complain that they get all the difficult ones. Each of them is generating their own responses.

Some sales assistants and customer care staff really do seem to get all the difficult, grumpy customers. If you watch, you'll observe that they are approaching their customers in a negative way. You have doubtless also observed that some children seem to have negative characteristics which echo their parents' behaviour. Perhaps the parents shout at the children frequently, and the children are loud and aggressive in turn. Maybe the parents never listen properly to their children, and then ask "Why does she never listen to what I'm saying?"

Of course, it's always easier to spot faults in other people than in ourselves. But most of us are guilty of generating negative behaviour in our children through behaving negatively towards them. We may not be as aggressive or as downright unpleasant as some parents, but we're not perfect either. More typical, everyday lapses include:

- Being faddy about food in front of the children, and then complaining when they won't eat their greens
- Interrupting our children when they are speaking, and then telling them not to interrupt when we speak to them
- Raising our voices as soon as we get angry, and then shouting "Don't yell!" at the children

Mind you, what we notice less often (at least in others) is that our children – like our customers – mirror our good behaviour too. The thing is, we are on our best behaviour with our customers, but not necessarily with our children. This is understandable; after all, if you were up for two hours in the night clearing up vomit caused by eating too many sweets, it probably wasn't your customers' fault, so why take it out on them? Your child, on the other hand, is probably *not* top of your list of 'people to be nice to today'. Nevertheless, it's in your own interests to treat them well, because they are more likely to respond in kind.

Whenever you notice a characteristic you don't care for in your child, it's always worth asking yourself whether perhaps you exhibit the same characteristic yourself (be honest, now). If you have more than one child, and they all exhibit the same charateristic, the evidence against you starts to look pretty strong. So if they always start shouting every time there's a disagreement between you, resist the temptation to shout back. Just say, firmly but without raising your voice, "I'm not shouting, so you don't need to either."

Treat the customer with respect

The technique: Customers should always be treated with politeness, deference and respect. That simply means remembering to say please and thank you to them, apologising for keeping them waiting, listening properly to what they are saying, and observing all those little niceties which make them feel that they are important to you.

This technique should be child's play with customers. And so it should with children, too. But for some reason we often drop these niceties at home. It's strange: treating someone with respect is a way of showing them that they are important. And who is more important to us than our children? And yet, perhaps because this behaviour seems somehow formal, we abandon it with the people who most deserve it.

Of course, this rule of customer care is linked to the previous one: your behaviour generates similar behaviour in return. If we don't treat our children with respect, it is rather hypocritical to complain when they show us no respect. So treating them respectfully is the best way to stop them telling you to "Shut up", or "Give me my clean socks now", or even simply ignoring you (I'm never sure which is worse).

The point to aim for is one where the family home echoes continually to the sound of pleases and thank yous, and phrases such as "Sorry to keep you waiting", "Excuse me", "Would you mind…", and "Can I give you a hand with that?" All right, perhaps that sounds a little implausible. But actually, it's not so difficult as you think. Just visualise a customer's face superimposed over your child's, and you'll find it's simply the behaviour you use every day at work.

Handle complaints effectively

Handling complaints at work means dealing with a dissatisfied customer in such a way that you leave them feeling not only satisfied but positively impressed with you and your organisation. The kind of complaints you might have to handle range from the minor gripe to the full on, claws out rant. But even the minor complaints would turn into major ones if you handled them badly.

Of course, children are much better at complaining than customers are. In fact, they make most customers look pathetic. Perhaps next time a customer says "Excuse me, sorry to bother you, but this toaster I bought from you yesterday doesn't seem to work and it's just set fire to my kitchen" the best response would be to say "Come on! You can do better than that. Wait there, and I'll just go and fetch a small child to show you how it *should* be done."

Since customers were all children once, I can only suppose that complaining is a skill most of us lose as we get older. Certainly we tend to make far fewer complaints as customers ourselves than we receive from our children. But the good news is that we can handle our children's complaints – whether they are expressed as little whinges or delivered at a hundred decibels accompanied by sobs and tears – in just the same way as we handle complaints from customers. It's just a matter of following the six key steps:

1 Listen
2 Sympathise
3 Don't get defensive
4 Ask questions
5 Involve the customer in the solution
6 Carry it out

Listen

The technique: The customer is never going to calm down until they have had their say, and got their feelings out into the open. So just listen until they have finished saying what they want to. You can help the listening process by asking them relevant questions to show you're interested, but don't make them feel rushed or pressured into shutting up or they'll become more frustrated.

It's often the case that, where your own child is concerned, you instantly know what the trouble is. But that's not the point – any more than it is with customers. Only half the point of listening is to establish the facts (at least as they see them). The other half is psychological: to allow them to let off steam, and to feel that you are paying attention to their complaint.

If you don't go through this process, your child (or customer) will carry on shouting: they still feel they need to make themselves heard. But once they feel confident that you are giving the matter the attention they feel it deserves (even if you privately disagree), they will have no need to shout. So the fastest way to calm them down – and prevent your nerves fraying any further – is to hear them out.

And once you've heard them, let them know you have. Otherwise they will keep repeating themselves until they think you've got it. So just summarise the problem and repeat it back to them: "You're not happy because it's macaroni cheese for supper and you don't like it. I understand now why you're upset."

Sympathise

The technique: Customers are often angry because they are on the defensive: they are worried you'll tell them it was all their fault for not reading the instructions properly, or that you'll look at the toaster and insist that there's nothing wrong with it. The quickest way to reassure them that you're on their side is to sympathise with them. This is not the same thing as apologising. You can say you're sorry something happened without saying it was your fault. Or commiserate with how frightening it must have been when the kitchen caught fire.

Children, like customers, are worried you're going to tell them it's all their fault, or that there's nothing to complain about. They're afraid you might say "Well, you ate it last time I gave it to you" (which may well be true), or "Nonsense! Macaroni cheese is good for you. Now just eat it up."

So the sooner you can reassure them that you're taking their complaint seriously, the sooner they will move on towards finding a solution and getting the whole thing over with. You can sympathise without apologising, of course. How about, "Oh no. So you hate macaroni cheese and this is the second time this week we've had it. You must be fed up to the back teeth."

Don't get defensive

The technique: Never try to justify your actions – it's really irritating to someone who's complaining. It makes them feel you're implying that they are exaggerating the scale of the problem. What's more, they're simply not interested in *your* side of it. All they care about is that their toaster isn't working. Once you've listened and sympathised you should find the customer is calming down nicely. Don't blow it all by saying, "Well, it's not our fault. We don't make these toasters, we only sell them on. If there's a problem, it's the manufacturer's fault."

Children are at least as single-minded – not to say self-centred – as grown-ups. Your eight year old doesn't care about your side of it, and is extremely unlikely to respond to your defensive comment of, "Well, I can't possibly remember all your likes and dislikes" with a conciliatory "Fair point. OK, I'll gag it down then. No problem."

So you may have a perfectly valid defence. Indeed, you may well be in the right. But the odds are that you're better off in the long run getting this outburst over with as quickly as possible, than pointlessly mounting a well argued defence that falls on deaf ears.

There is one other point here. I hate to say this, but it's just possible that your child may be right. It almost never happens I know, but maybe, just once in a blue moon... What if it is the second time this week you've given them macaroni cheese? And what if your eight year old *did* tell you on Tuesday that he didn't like it?

There is a simple rule about apologising: never apologise if it isn't your fault, but always apologise if it is. This applies to customers too (legal requirements allowing) so, assuming your son isn't going to sue you for serving up a meal you knew he didn't like, why not apologise?

We frequently demand apologies from our children – for being cheeky, for hitting their brother or sister, for snatching. But how often do we set an example ourselves by apologising when we're in the wrong? We are often even more defensive than they are. So if it's your fault, swallow your pride and say so. Your children will respect you for it (although they'll never admit it).

Ask questions

The technique: It's time to get on with resolving the complaint. So the next stage is to ask questions in order to help identify the options for putting things right. Your questions aim to identify what happened in order to shed light on the problem. Was it the plug or the toaster itself which ignited? Were there any other problems? You're not trying to allocate blame – we've already established you don't want to do that – but you need information. There's no point sending the toaster off for repairs if a new plug will fix the problem.

Find out as much as you can about your child's problem. Bear in mind that cross-examination can make children feel nervous, so ask in a tone of concerned interest, don't do an impression of the Spanish inquisition. If serving up macaroni cheese is going to be a problem in future, you need to find out precisely why before you can suggest a workable alternative. So ask questions such as "Is it the macaroni or the cheese you don't like?" and "Can you manage to eat it this time if I stop cooking it so often in future?" and "What *do* you particularly like?"

Asking questions has the added benefit of demonstrating a genuine concern to resolve the problem. If you're handling this complaint according to the rules so far, you should find that any initial flood of noise and anger has by now slowed to a mere trickle.

Involve the customer in the solution

The technique: Your customer came to you because they wanted a solution to their problem. Sure, they may also have wanted to let off steam, but in the end they want to resolve the problem. So you need to find an answer. But it needs to be one your customer feels involved in, so that they will support it and go along with it. This means they have to choose the solution themselves. So offer them a choice of options, and let *them* have the final say. You could, for example, offer to repair the toaster, exchange it for another, or give them a refund.

One technique that works with customers is to ask them, "What would you like us to do to resolve this?" However, you should avoid this if you have one of those occasional customers who is still annoyed enough to be unreasonable and ask for the moon. "I'd like you to replace this toaster with your top of the range model. And I'd like you to pay for the repairs to the damaged plug socket, and for an entire kitchen refit as well." If this is likely to happen, don't ask. Just offer them a choice of two or three more realistic options.

The same goes for children, but there's a higher chance of them asking for something totally unrealistic. A three year old might well insist: "I don't ever, ever want you to cook anything ever again without asking me first, even if it's for somebody else." Of course, the older they are the more reasonable they become – but only slightly. So judge their mood; you know your own child. But if you're in doubt, don't give them free range to pick the solution of their choice.

It's not generally difficult to come up with more than one route for them to choose between. For example: "What if I cooked some cauliflower to pour your cheese sauce over while everyone else has macaroni? Or could you stomach macaroni cheese if I make it no more than once a month?"

Carry it out

The technique: If you say you'll do something, you'd better make sure you do it. And get it right. Otherwise you'll blow all the good work you've just done, and your customer will be twice as angry as they were last time – and justifiably so. So check the toaster is repaired properly if that's the option the customer picks, and make sure it's returned to them promptly and in proper working order this time.

You don't need me to tell you what will happen if you serve your eight year old macaroni cheese again next week. If you say you'll do something, you'd better make sure you remember. Don't commit yourself in the first place to anything you can't promise to fulfil. You may have a sneaking suspicion that he doesn't really mind macaroni cheese that much anyway, but he *does* mind you treating him as though he's so unimportant you can't remember your promises to him.

Summary

It should be clear by now that practising customer care skills on your kids will bring the same rewards it does when you use them on your customers. And complaint handling for children is just the same as complaint handling for customers, whether it's a meal they don't like again, or whether you always make them sit in the middle of the back seat of the car, or whether you promised you'd mend their doll's house and you still haven't.

There's only one significant difference between customers and children when it comes to complaints: 96 percent of unhappy customers don't bother to complain. If only children were the same…

Selling skills: get your children to do whatever you want... willingly

Customer relations made sense, but selling skills? Why do you need selling skills to bring up children? Well it's true that they're not likely to be in the market for any products or services you sell at work – and if they were it would probably be your money they'd be spending anyway. You certainly need to be able to sell them ideas, though.

It's not money you want them to part with, of course – that would be too easy. No, this is far more of a challenge. You want them to co-operate with you. You want to sell them the idea of eating their breakfast, or having their room painted blue instead of flourescent pink, or getting in the car to go to the shops.

Selling an idea is no different from selling a product or a service. If you're used to writing proposals or giving presentations – both of which aim to sell ideas – you'll know that it's the same thing in essence. Certainly the techniques which work are the same ones. And the good news is that they work just as well on children as they do on customers.

The only thing that differs is the idea you're trying to sell. You don't often find yourself selling a customer the idea of finishing up their main course nicely before they can have any pudding (although feel free to try it if you like next time you take a customer out for a business lunch). Then again, children aren't necessarily difficult to sell to. You'd probably find it much harder to sell your customers the idea of fishing for leeches by holding their arm underwater in a stagnant pond until the leeches stick to it (a bizarre activity I enthusiastically indulged in as a child).

But selling is selling, and whether it's kids or customers, you still have to follow the same basic principles:

1. Set your objective
2. Prepare alternatives
3. Ask open ended questions
4. Keep control
5. Sell benefits, not features
6. Handle any objections
7. Close the sale

Set your objective

The technique: Before you launch into a sale, you need to know what you're trying to achieve – or how will you know if you've been successful? If you manufacture nails and screws to sell to hardware retailers, you won't be happy if you sell just three nails. You'll be aiming to sell, for example, 15 boxes. If you sell grand country houses, on the other hand, you'll be happy simply to sell the idea of taking a look around – an appointment to view – at your first contact. Whichever it is, set your objective before you start.

Children are very good at arguing you out of things – or at least trying to – or simply wearing you down by attrition. Unless you're very certain what you're trying to achieve before you start, you have no hope of achieving it by the end of the arguing and procrastinating and general resistance. You do have one advantage when it comes to selling to children, however. At least you know when you're going to have to work hard to make a sale. (As a general rule of thumb the answer is always.) This means that at least you have an opportunity to prepare.

And the first stage of preparation is to establish firmly in your own mind what it is that you intend to achieve. You need to be realistic, of course. A jumbo jet salesperson doesn't expect to clinch the deal on 25 aeroplanes at the first meeting with the airline buyer. And you can't expect to get your child to tidy their room, change the bed, do all their homework, have a bath and be sitting at the table ready when you put the dinner down on it. On a bad day, you can't even expect one of these things. So be sensible in your objective.

Once you've set your objective, you must hold unwaveringly to it, otherwise your child will know they've got the better of you. And once they know that's possible, they won't rest until they get the better of you next time and every time. Suppose the kids are getting fractious and irritable because they've been cooped up in the house all morning. Your objective might be: *To get everyone to go out for the afternoon* (no matter what, or you'll go mad).

Prepare alternatives

The technique: Of course, you may not manage to sell what you hoped. But that doesn't mean the encounter with the customer has to be a dead loss. Just make sure you have prepared a fall back position. If you can't sell 15 boxes of nails, you'd settle for 15 boxes on sale or return. If you can't get an appointment to view, at least you can get the customer to agree to look at a copy of the particulars for the property. If you're smart, you'll have a 'hierarchy of objectives': sell 15 boxes, or sell 15 on sale or return, or sell 10 boxes, or sell five, or leave a sample and make a follow-up appointment.

Perhaps you reckon it would be a good idea to get everyone out to the park for the afternoon, so they can burn off some of that excess energy, and you won't have to do too much yourself. Just sit on a bench and keep an eye on them. (Who are you kidding?) So that's your top choice.

But it's not the only option which would meet your objective. And if it meets resistance, you'll need other options at the ready. Otherwise the choice will be to give in (and be seen to give in) by staying at home, or physically drag them to the park if necessary. Hobson's choice.

Make life easy on yourself. Line up some other possibilities which still meet your overall objective. Maybe you could sell them the idea of taking the dog for a walk. Or you could even go shopping. It's harder work for you, but there's more opportunity for bribing them into behaving well. (Pretend I didn't say that.)

Ask open ended questions

The technique: When you're trying to make a sale, you want the customer to do most of the talking. You need to find out what they want from the product, what would be the plus and minus points, before you can know what to offer them. So collect information by asking questions, such as "What size house would you be looking for? How many bedrooms?" And show you're listening to the answers.

Many parents make the mistake at this point of simply announcing what's going to happen. "Right, everyone, we're off to the park now." (Which you might as well follow up by saying, "Right, everyone. I've backed myself into a corner now.") Even if you're happy to walk the dog, it's going to look like backing down if you agree to it now.

Of course, there are times when there isn't a choice – or there isn't much choice. But you can still approach the sale by asking questions. For one thing, it makes the children feel they have had a say in the final outcome. And for another thing, it gives you ammunition for making the prospect sound more attractive.

And that's the real point of asking questions. When you ask a customer what they are looking for, you do it so that you can tailor your offer to their exact requirements. But if you sell nails and screws, you're obviously not going to end up offering them a box of hammers and two dozen staple guns. Your choice of questions will keep the conversation within the relevant limits.

So what questions are you going to ask your children? Well, the ones you want the answers to, basically. "How do you feel about going out?" "Where would you like to go?" "How about playing on the swings?" "Would you like to take Rover for a walk?" Gauge your questions according to the answers you get. Don't mention the shops if you think you can get away without, but bring them into play if it looks necessary. You're using their answers to assess which is your most likely chance of a sale. Is the customer more likely to want the six inch nails or the four inch ones? Are the kids more likely to agree to go to the park or take the dog out?

Obviously, it's possible that the kids might all respond instantly with "Oh yes, the park would be great. Please, *please* take us to the park and we promise to be good all day long." Then again, maybe you live in the real world. Either way, asking questions can only help you to judge where your best prospects of a sale are, rather than launching straight into it without finding out what your customer wants first.

Keep control

The technique: Some customers seem to take over the sales conversation and end up cross-examining you about your products or services.

You: "What kind of property are you looking for?"

Customer: "What sort of properties have you got?"

You: "We sell at the top end of the market, luxury country houses."

Customer: "How many have you got on your books at the moment?"

You: "About 12."

Customer: "Is that all?"

Now, whose in charge of that conversation? You can keep control by answering any questions with a question of your own.

Customer: "What sort of properties have you got?"

You: "What price range are you interested in?"

It's true that customers sometimes take over a sales conversation, but at least they observe common courtesies. Children, on the other hand, feel no such compunction. So they are much more likely to try to take over and railroad you into an alternative option of their choice. They'll start on "Why can't we stay here?" and "If you want us to go out, why don't we all go to the cinema?"

Of course, once in a while they will inadvertently come out with a suggestion which you are perfectly happy with. If this happens, don't miss your chance. Say a brief prayer of thanks and grab the opportunity – it doesn't happen often. It's like a customer walking in and saying "You've got some nice properties in your portfolio. I'll take this one. Oh, and I'll have this one as well."

More often, they will challenge your questions with their own. "Why the park?" In that case, don't get into an argument; simply respond with a question of your own, so that you keep control of the conversation. For example: "Don't you like the park?" If they say "No", ask them "What don't you like about it?" You may not be getting their agreement yet, but that bit comes later. For now, you're collecting information. If they say they don't like the swings, that still gives you the option of going over to the river on the other side of the park. If they've become allergic to grass since this morning, however, the trip to the park is out of the running.

Sell benefits, not features

The technique: Don't tell the customer what your product can do, but what it can do *for them*. Don't say "The dining room measures 20 feet by 15 feet", say "The dining room is very large, so there's plenty of room to entertain your friends and family." Always express any feature of the product or service in terms of the benefits it will bring to the customer.

Children are even more self-centred than customers. It's not their fault – it's just the way they see the world. Very small children actually believe the world revolves around them. That's why, instead of saying, "Look at the moon!" a two year old will often say, "The moon's looking at me!" It's not just a figure of speech, it's what they really believe. It takes children about 18 years to grow out of this fully (that's a minimum), so it's no surprise that even much older children see the world from their own perspective.

So if you want to persuade your five or six year old to go to the park – or to do anything else – it's not going to work unless you talk in terms of what's in it for them. It's no good saying "There's plenty of fresh air at the park," or "It will occupy most of the afternoon fairly painlessly." Put it in terms that a five year old can relate to: "Your dolls could do with a walk in the fresh air," or "You can see how fast you can get the roundabout to spin round without falling off it," or "We might see the squirrels again, like we did last time."

Talking in terms of benefits and not features really isn't difficult. You simply have to put yourself in your customer's – or child's – shoes. It's as easy with a 15 year old as it is with a five year old. Suppose you want your teenager to tidy their room: "You'll qualify for your bonus pocket money if you do it," or "There'll be much more space for your leech collection if you clear the desk," or even – to get right inside the mind of what appeals to a teenager – "I'll stop nagging you if you do it."

Handle any objections

However well you sell a product, a service or an idea, your customer (or your child) may still have reservations about it. It's too expensive, it will take too long, they're not sure the colour is right, or whatever. So you need to be able to respond to these objections in a way which will persuade the customer that they are unfounded, or at least that they are outweighed by the benefits. There is a three stage approach for doing this:

1. Get them to be specific
2. Put the objection into context
3. Give compensating factors

Get them to be specific

The technique: Get your customer to make their objection as specific as possible (in other words, know your enemy). Ask them "How much did you expect to pay?" or "How quickly do you need it?"

If (or should I say when) your child objects to your proposal, you can't just cave in. You could switch from suggesting to ordering – or even threatening – but the tone of the encounter will change for the worse, and the next hour or two could be unpleasant to live through. Far better to find a way to counter the objection. So when your five year old says "I don't like going to the park", get them to be more specific. "What don't you like about it?"

Once you know what you're dealing with, it makes things much easier. But if you don't ask them to be specific, you won't know. And the younger they are, the more true this is. Very small children sometimes have the most unexpected reasons for objecting, and you have no chance of guessing what they are. Perhaps one of the trees is in a shape which looks like a scary face, or maybe they once saw a dog in the park which barked and made them jump. No, you can't possibly know what you're up against if you don't ask.

You might suppose that your five year old thinks the swings are boring and would rather stay home and play or watch television. But if you ask her, you may get a different answer altogether, such as, "It's a very long walk to get there." That's fine – we can deal with that, now we know what the problem is.

Put the objection into context

The technique: Show the customer why – looked at in the context – the problem isn't so great. "Remember that the price includes delivery and installation costs", or "We build it to order, and then test it rigorously, so three weeks is pretty swift really, if you think about it."

She's probably right – it probably is a long walk (at least to her). So you can't show her she's got the facts wrong. What you need to do is to put the length of the walk in context: "It's about 10 minutes each way, but we'll stay for a couple of hours. So we'll spend most of the time playing in the park."

This works for just about anything. Let's take your reluctant teenager who doesn't want to tidy his bedroom. If you ask him why not and he tells you it's so boring, try saying: "Parts of it are boring, but you'll find all sorts of interesting things under the bed and down the back of the chair cushions. You might even find that CD you lost a couple of weeks ago." (Whatever you do, resist the temptation to point out that it's a lot less boring than sitting around doing nothing, which is how he spends the rest of his free time if he's a normal teenager.)

Give compensating factors

The technique: You can extend the compensations beyond the immediate context, to other factors: "It's not the cheapest on the market, I grant you, but it will last you much longer than a cheaper version (putting it in context). And you'll be the envy of your neighbours (other compensating factor)."

Don't limit yourself to pointing out directly relevant factors which compensate. That's the first stage – to address their immediate objection. But once you've done that, round it off by pointing out all the other benefits as well. So you can tell your five year old: "It's about 10 minutes each way, but we'll stay for a couple of hours. So we'll spend most of the time playing in the park. And you can have a go on that new climbing frame they've just built."

As for your teenager: "Parts of it are boring, but you'll find all sorts of interesting things under the bed and down the back of the chair cushions. And once you've just helped me with Friday's shopping as well as tidying your room, you'll have earned yourself an extra £5 bonus pocket money."

Close the sale

Closing the sale with a customer is all about getting them to say yes. This can mean handing over the cash, signing the contract, submitting the purchase order or simply shaking on the deal.

Getting your child to say yes may be tough, but in the end the same techniques will win through. And once you've mastered closing the sale with your own children, customers will seem a doddle by comparison. (Except that it's harder to bribe customers successfully with the promise of a tube of Smarties.)

If you're used to selling, you may well already know many of the standard techniques for closing. If you've laid the groundwork properly, as we saw earlier, you will already have made the offer or product appealing, and dealt with any objections your customer or child may have had. So all you need to do now is to get them to commit themselves.

Customers often need prompting to do this because they are waiting for you to take the initiative, or perhaps because they are just nervous of committing the budget in case the boss thinks they've made a stupid decision. Children don't usually care what the boss thinks (in other words, you) and they have no qualms about overspending budgets if they think they can get away with it. They resist for other reasons.

Most often, if you've laid the groundwork well, the problem is that although you've convinced them in principle, your timing and theirs don't agree. Just because it's worth tidying their bedroom in exchange for extra pocket money, doesn't mean to say they want to do it now.

If your child happens to be two, bad luck. Two year olds (as you may not need telling) think lots of things are a good idea, but they never want to stop what they're doing at the moment. They have a 'jam tomorrow' mentality – they'll do something different tomorrow and something different yesterday, but they'll never do anything different today. However, if the shopping needs doing now because you're out of milk, bread and even spaghetti hoops, you need your child to agree to get in the car now and not tomorrow.

So here are four of the top techniques for closing the sale, along with guidelines on how to apply them to your own children. If any of these techniques don't work, you haven't necessarily failed. Just make sure there are no outstanding objections and then try another technique.

The assumptive close

The technique: This is a very simple approach: just take the sale for granted. In business terms this means saying: "That'll be £12.99 then" for example, or "I'll put you down for three green ones in the large size. Could you just sign here, please?"

When it comes to children, the key to this technique is timing. You've been through the selling process, you've dealt with any objections, now get in there fast before they have time to notice you're doing it. The second they have implied agreement, or run out of objections, grab your opportunity. Don't wait for them to say 'yes' (or 'yuh' or 'uh-huh' or whatever noises some children use to indicate assent).

Once you've persuaded your reluctant teenager (with or without the use of bribery) that they should be doing more of the household chores, simply say "I'll draw up a rota, and then you can check it to make sure it's fair." Now leave the room quickly. You may not have won the war (what are the chances, frankly, that they'll think it's a fair rota?) but you have won the battle. It is now taken as read that they will do more chores; you're down to discussing details.

The alternative close

The technique: A nice easy one this. Don't ask them if they want the product, just say "Do you want it in red or blue?" or "Do you want to take 20 this time, or would you like to start with 10?" In other words, give the customer options which don't include saying no to the purchase.

This works with children of any age, but it works particularly well with small children. It's a form of railroading, although obviously that's not something you'd ever do to your children. Perhaps it's better to see it as giving them a choice. And that is a lot of the reason why it works with small children: they like to feel that they have some control over their lives, and this technique appears to give it to them.

The only thing is, *you're* controlling the options. But they are genuinely making the final choice. Instead of saying to your two year old "Put your shoes on, we're going to the park", you let *them* choose where to go, from a selection which you have already edited: "We're going out. Would you like to go to the park or take the dog for a walk?" Whichever they choose, the point is that they have unwittingly agreed to go out.

Since small children can be perverse, a useful variation on this technique involves making out that you have a preferred option. They will take great delight in choosing to go to the park after your mock protestations of "Please don't make me go all the way to the park; choose dog walking, *please*". If you actually have a preference, and you're smart, you'll pretend to hate the one you secretly prefer. (By the way, this variation will not go on working until they are 18. They'll see through it eventually.)

The question close

The technique: Use this in response to a question, when the question appears to represent any outstanding objections. If a customer asks: "Do you do it in black?" you reply, "You'd like it in black, would you?" When they say yes, they have effectively agreed to the sale.

One of the advantages of this approach is that even when your children come to recognise it, they still have to go along with it. It is a sort of variation on 'when did you stop beating your wife?' In fact, if your child doesn't want you to use this technique on them, they will have to avoid asking the question in the first place. Once they have – and you've learnt to spot the moment – they are hoist by their own petard (which is apparently an explosive device, and nothing to do with flags at all. So to extend the metaphor: if they ask you a suitable question, you've got them bang to rights).

The key here is recognising your opportunity and pouncing on it. So here are a couple of examples of the kind of questions children can scupper themselves with, and the response you need to use to clinch the deal:

Q: "Can I go on the swings at the park?"
A: "Do you want to go on the swings?"

Q: "Can Emily come back to stay for the night?"
A: "If Emily comes back with you, do you promise to be home by 10?"

The puppydog close

The technique: The name of this technique for closing the sale becomes obvious once you know how it works. It operates on the principle of 'try it, and if you don't like it you can always change your mind'. As in "Just take this cute little puppy home for a week, and if you don't want the little chap after that, you can bring him back." It is the basis of the '30 days' free trial' type of selling.

This works if you're sure your child will enjoy something, but you can't quite persuade them of it in advance. It's a good one to use on your two year old who never wants to do anything other than what they are doing now. Try saying: "We'll just go to the park for 10 minutes and if you don't want to stay after that, we'll come straight home."

It works well on older children too, who recognise a certain fairness in it (compared with "Just DO IT!"). It makes them feel that you are giving them ultimate control, so long as they just make this little concession of trying it out for a bit first. The only thing is, you have to stick to your side of it. If they really don't like it once they've tried it, you have to accept no for an answer. Otherwise they won't trust you next time, and you won't be able to use the technique again.

Summary

Selling to children is great practice for selling to customers. The techniques are the same, but you're playing for higher stakes. For one thing, children are more honest. A customer might say "Thanks, but I don't think I will", where a child will tell you *exactly* what they think of your idea – and where you can stick it – if you haven't sold it well.

What's more, the worst that can happen if it goes wrong with a customer is that you lose a sale. But if you fail to sell an idea to your kids… instead of an afternoon in the park you could have to spend the next four hours playing 'Ken and Barbie go to the shops'.

Negotiating skills: meet each other half way

Now here's a collection of skills we all recognise as being important when it comes to children. There are times as a parent when family life seems to be one long round of negotiations (commonly termed 'arguments'). And the older children get, the less responsive they become to being told to go and do something without debate. An 18 month old might happily eat whatever you put in front of them, but a 10 year old is likely to launch into a lengthy bartering session about exactly how much salad they have to eat before they're allowed a bowl of ice cream afterwards.

Negotiating is often seen as a more specialised business skill than, say, good customer relations or even selling. But in fact all the guidelines for successful negotiating are simple to follow even if you haven't formally learnt them before. And as soon as you understand them, you realise that most of negotiating is about psychology.

One of the most important psychological aspects of negotiation is that you need to keep your bargaining tools under your hat (if you'll pardon the metaphor). Don't let the other side find out what you're prepared to settle for, or what concessions you're prepared to make. Otherwise they'll beat you down and give you nothing in return. So don't reveal more than you need to, but always try to find out as much as you can about *their* bargaining position – it's all valuable ammunition.

Negotiating may be about trying to score points at each other's expense, but in business the aim is always to do it in an atmosphere of pleasant civility. You might bitch and moan privately about the other lot, but to their face you should always be polite and friendly. Occasionally this breaks down, but it doesn't help the negotiation when it happens. More often, there is a genuine willingness to please. The other side, after all, are only doing the same thing as you: trying to get the best deal they can.

Where children are involved, the aim should be the same. As soon as tempers start to rise, your child will develop a strong desire not only to get what they want from the negotiation, but also to grind you into the dirt in the process. Since children are natural negotiators (as you won't need telling) there is a good chance they will succeed. At the very least, you probably won't get what you want from the deal. So keep things sweet as far as you can, for your own sake and for the sake of reaching a workable negotiated solution.

Negotiate a win/win deal

The technique: Everyone goes into a negotiation wanting to clinch a good deal, which will necessarily have to be at the expense of the other side. In other words, they treat it as a battle, and one which they want to win. So the trick is to make the other side feel they've won, while also coming out feeling that *you've* won. It's known as win/win negotiating. The way to do it is to ask for more than you want (or offer less than you really intend), and then let them beat you down to the level you were actually expecting to settle for all along. They think they've won, but you've got exactly what you want, too.

Most children have healthy egos, and they don't want to lose face. If your negotiation tactics leave them feeling they've lost and it shows, they are unlikely to come to an agreement. Then you're back to enforcing the rule of law, which is far less effective. Negotiated agreements are better than enforced submissions for several reasons:

- They avoid stressful and unpleasant encounters
- Everyone feels successful and positive
- The agreement has the support of both sides, so you are both much more likely to stick to it

Of course, there aren't enough hours in the day to enter full scale negotiations over every little thing, right down to whether they get dressed before or after they clean their teeth. But neither should there be any call to. The win/win approach is useful in the briefest of informal negotiations, when your child probably doesn't even realise they're negotiating at all.

Suppose your small child asks to play with their new toy for a bit after supper, instead of going straight to bed. If you're smart, you'll decide how long an extension they can have, and then offer them less – give them room to win a negotiation. So you say: "OK, but only 10 minutes." They say (as you knew they would): "Oh, please, can I have 20 minutes?" You can then settle for 20 – or even meet in the middle at 15. Either way, you've just held a successful win/win negotiation in the space of a few seconds.

In order to come up with a win/win solution, you have to be able to look at the problem from their point of view. The odds are that your child will be more than happy to fill you in on the way they see things, but make an effort to appreciate it, rather than simply hear them out because you feel you should. If you really understand things from their side, you are likely to be more willing to make concessions.

Imagine your 14 year old daughter wants to go out to a

disco and come back at 11.30 at night on the bus. You think this is far too late and an unsafe way to travel (especially given what she'll probably want to wear). But listen to her point of view: all her friends will be there, and she'll feel really stupid if she's the only one whose parents won't let her go.

Come on. Don't you remember being 14? It's humiliating when your parents won't let you join in with what everyone else is doing. You may still not agree to the arrangements as they stand, but once you see her point of view, don't you feel more inclined to co-operate? Wouldn't you like her to feel that she's won an agreement from you that she's happy with?

Why not let her go to the disco but make the finish time a little earlier? And you could pick her up in the car. You've got what you want – you feel she's safe – and she's got what she wanted: she gets to go to the disco. So everyone can leave the negotiation feeling successful.

There's just one essential rule for win/win negotiating with your children: you must never, ever let them know your technique. Their satisfaction lies in knowing that you've lost, you've got egg all over your face, they handled the negotiation better than you and you're wishing you'd never agreed to bargain in the first place. If you ever let them find out that none of these is the case, you will have thrown away one of their biggest incentives to reach a mutual agreement – the satisfaction of beating you. So keep it to yourself. When they've grown up, left home and entered the world of business, they may finally learn the rules of negotiating and recognise your tactics. But by then it won't matter any more.

Know your bottom line

The technique: In every negotiation, there is a theoretical point below which the deal stops being worthwhile. Suppose you're negotiating to sell your products to a large customer for a bulk discount. You've done your figures, and you know that you'd be happy to give them a 10 percent discount, but you'd settle for 15. More than 20 percent, however, and the deal just isn't worth having. So 20 percent is your absolute bottom line.

If you go into a deal without knowing your bottom line, there is nothing to stop your child bargaining you down to the point where the deal just isn't worth it. If you haven't set your bottom line, you won't recognise this point. Sooner or later, of course, you'll realise you've stepped beyond it, but by then it will be too late.

Suppose your nine year old is haggling with you for a later bedtime. You're suggesting 9 o'clock, but they think it should be 10.30. Before you know where you are, you've agreed to 10 o'clock. After you've had a chance to think about it, you're really not happy with this at all. However, there's nothing you can do about it. Do you really want to go back and tell your nine year old that you're reneging on the agreement? And do you honestly fancy your chances of getting away with it? As far as children are concerned, a deal is a deal – at least when it's in their favour.

The thing to do is to decide before you start negotiating exactly how late is the latest you'll agree to. Maybe it's 9.30. In the interests of win/win negotiating you can start by offering 9 o'clock. That way they'll feel they've won when you finally agree to 9.30. Who knows, they might even settle for 9 o'clock without fuss (and pigs might fly).

And what, you might be wondering, are you supposed to do when you have to think on your feet? Smart children spring these negotiations on you when you least expect it because they know their chances of success are better if they catch you on the hop. So they wait until you're preoccupied helping their little brother with his homework at the same time as getting supper ready, feeding the dog and preparing the packed lunches for school tomorrow. Then they nonchalantly enquire, "Don't you think it's time my bedtime was a bit later? All my friends go to bed at about 10.30." You're supposed to say "Do they, darling? Oh, fair enough then."

No, no, no! Don't let them get the better of you like this. Even if you've got the sense to argue the case rather than simply capitulating, it still won't do. You wouldn't let a customer get away with it, so don't let your child do it either. If a customer called you in the middle of a meeting and started trying to negotiate a deal with you, you'd say "I'm afraid I'm in a meeting at the moment, and I can't give this the attention it deserves. Can I call you back this afternoon?" Or even, "Can I call you later to make an appointment to come and see you so we can discuss it?"

So do the same with children: "Sorry, but I'm very busy at the moment. Let's talk about it later, when I can give you my full attention." That should stop their little game, while sounding completely co-operative and willing to negotiate. Don't talk on their terms, wait until you can do it on your own terms. Now you've bought time to sit down and think through the issue, and decide what your bottom line is before negotiations begin.

You may not need to fix a bottom line for tiny, everyday negotiations, such as whether or not they have to eat everything on their plate (though once you get into the habit it comes quickly and naturally even for these quick deals). But if the results of the agreement are going to last into the future – such as bedtimes, pocket money, or anything which sets a precedent – always know your bottom line before you agree to start talking.

There are two important points to remember about your bottom line:

1. Never let the ~~enemy~~ child find out what your bottom line is. Otherwise they won't settle for anything less.
2. Never claim to have reached your bottom line unless you have, or you'll be crying wolf. If you say "That's absolutely as far as I can go", you'd better mean it. If you let them beat you down further, they won't believe you next time you say it, even if it's true. And that leads to stalemate.

Aim high

The technique: A successful negotiation depends on having room for manoeuvre. If neither of you is prepared to budge from your starting position, you haven't got the basis for a negotiation at all. And your room for manoeuvre is the space between what you start off asking for, and the bottom line you'd be prepared to settle for. So the higher you aim initially, the more scope for negotiating you have… and the better chance that you will never have to drop as low as your bottom line. So if you can afford an absolute maximium discount of 20 percent, don't start by offering 18 percent. Start with 10 percent and give yourself plenty of negotiating ground.

Your son's fifth birthday is coming up, and he wants to invite all his school friends to a big party. Your personal preference is for taking him out for a treat on his own. Or, failing that, getting someone else to host the party so you can leave the country for a few hours. You're going to have to negotiate how many people he can invite.

You'll have to think about this one first, and decide what your bottom line is. Perhaps you feel you can just about cope with eight of the brats running around for the afternoon. But you can't start by offering him eight, or you have no room to give any ground – and that's not a negotiation. Besides, just because you can stand eight, doesn't mean you wouldn't be happier with six.

So aim high. If you can, find out how many he wants to invite (he may be unpractised enough in negotiating to reveal this information). You often tend to meet in the middle on this kind of deal, so if you know how many he wants, you can try to make sure eight is the middle point. If he has a list of 10, you can stipulate a maximum of six. Then you can meet in the middle at eight. If his list has 12 names on it and you start out saying six, you can't arrive at eight unless he gives more ground than you do. And how easy will that be to negotiate? So if he wants 12, you can start at four. And if you give other concessions too (as we'll see later), you might end up with even fewer than eight.

Yes, I realise that if he wants to invite 20 friends this system isn't going to be foolproof. But the odds are that he knows perfectly well 20 is unrealistic. And, as we'll see, there are other variables you can bring into play. If you have no idea how many people he wants to invite, and you can't wheedle a figure out of him – simply aim high. Suggest he invites his two or three closest friends and be prepared to give a fair bit of ground if you have to.

Remember that you need to start by aiming high, because once you've agreed to lower your demands, you can't raise them again. Imagine saying to an employee in the middle of negotiating their pay rise, "Sorry, but actually I can't offer you that five percent pay rise I said I could after all. Three percent is my absolute limit." It's just not on. You can't promise your son seven friends at his party and then reduce it to four later. Your life wouldn't be worth living.

So the one remaining question is: how high should you aim? And the answer is simple. As high as you can justify. If you ask your boss to draft in five extra staff to help you cover the exhibition next month, you know you have to be able to justify why you need five rather than only three or four. Well, the same goes here. How few friends can you justify allowing your son to invite? Think about other parties he's been to, or what he wants this party to entail, and decide what you can get away with.

It's the same with your nine year old's bedtime. You'll have a hard time justifying a bedtime of 6.30, but consider when their older siblings go to bed, what time they have to get up in the mornings, what time they go to bed now, and come up with the earliest bedtime you can reasonably justify. You're being kind really – you're giving them the chance to beat you down even further.

Look for variables

The technique: If you have only one factor to consider, such as money, you're not really negotiating at all. You're haggling. You offer 10 thousand, they say they'll take 12, you suggest 11 thousand and it's a deal. But a negotiation is more subtle and complex because you can bring in other factors, or variables. Suppose they say they'll take 12 thousand, and you say you'll give them 11 if they can deliver within three weeks. Now you're juggling cost and delivery time, and you're into a true negotiation. The more of these variables you can find, the more bargaining levers you have.

It's always worth bringing in as many variables as you can to a negotiation, especially if you haven't much room for manoeuvre on the central point at issue. If bedtime is currently 9 o'clock and you're really not prepared to move far on it at all, it will help if you can introduce other factors. Maybe you can offer a later bedtime at weekends and in the holidays, or perhaps you could let them leave the light on until 10 o'clock. Or let them have one later night each week if there's a particular television programme they want to watch. You could even offer to throw in a new set of more grown-up bedding (covered in footballers rather than elephants).

You can be as creative as you like. So long as you can make offers which will appeal to your child, any variable factor like this can help to clinch a deal. If you have both reached your bottom line and still haven't met in the middle, variables can be the only way to find a workable solution. The thing is, the variables can influence the bottom line. You're still set on a 9.30 bedtime, but it doesn't have to apply at weekends. They still want to go to bed at 10, but might concede four out of five weekdays.

One of the advantages of variables, however, is that they often help you to avoid ever reaching your bottom line. With no other bargaining points in play, you might have to let your five year old push you to letting him invite eight friends to his party. But introduce variables to the negotiation, and you may well keep him to fewer. For example:

- For every person he knocks off his invitation list, you'll add £20 to the budget for the party (if you're going to use bribery, you might as well be creative with it)
- If there are no more than two friends (let him negotiate you up to three here) you'll take them all out for a special treat such as the circus or a pantomime
- The fewer party guests, the longer the party can go on (put it this way to be positive, rather than saying the more there are, the shorter it will have to be)
- He can have eight people on the condition that none of them is either Jim or Matt, each of whom count as two people (and that's being generous)

Anything which will help you to reach an agreement is OK. It doesn't have to have anything to do with the matter under negotiation, so long as you are both prepared to bargain with it. So you might say that if he limits the number of friends he invites, you'll have his bike resprayed the colour he keeps asking you to.

You can be endlessly creative with variables once you get into practice. Here's another standard negotiation which all of us have to hold with our children sooner or later: pocket money. Instead of simply haggling, think of some more variables:

- Half their pocket money is sacrosanct, the other half has to be earned by doing chores
- They can't have the raise they want, but you'll give them a book allowance every month as well
- Pocket money can go up, but they have to save a percentage of it towards more expensive items which you approve (they can always save the rest of it towards things you don't approve)

...and so on. I'm sure you've got the idea.

Just don't limit yourself. You have far more scope when it comes negotiating with your children than with your customers or your boss, because you should have a much better idea of what will motivate them, even if it's unrelated to the subject under discussion. After all, you can't generally sway a customer by saying "Oh, and if you'll settle for a 15 percent discount, I'll take you camping on Saturday night."

Get all their cards on the table

The technique: Some people go into negotiations with the intention of being underhand, and tricking you into giving away more than you meant to. The classic technique for doing this is to wait until you've almost agreed the deal and then throw something new onto the table.

Perhaps you've already said you can give them a 15 percent discount, and then they announce that they also need delivery within a fortnight. It's too late to use this as a bargaining lever, because you've committed to the discount. The way to prevent this is to agree a list of factors at issue before you begin. That way, they can't reasonably introduce anything new at the last minute – and if they do, you can justifiably refuse to discuss it without going back over other factors.

I'm sure your child is an honest, fair-minded, open person who would be horrified at the mere thought of employing any kind of underhand tactics. Well, maybe with someone else. But parents are different – they're fair game. Your child can get all their Machiavellian tendencies out of their system on you, so that everyone else can get the benefit of the honest, decent side of their nature. Everyone, that is, except you – you, who did all the hard work of making them fair and honest in the first place.

Face it. When they're negotiating with you, your child can be as underhand, cheating and manipulative as everyone else's. And it's only a matter of time before they work out (if they haven't already) that the smart way to get what they want is to conceal half their demands until you've all but agreed the first half. Even if you feel you haven't committed yourself yet, you've still revealed what you're prepared to settle for.

So don't tell your five year old that he can have six people to his party, and then have him announce that he wants to take everyone to the movies. If you'd known that, you'd have limited the numbers to three or four. You will often find that if you think about it, you can work out what a lot of your child's demands are likely to be. You could have guessed, really, that your son would want to discuss the activities at the party sooner or later.

The answer is to treat your child as you would a customer you were negotiating with, or an employee. Begin by saying, "Let's make a list of everything that either of us wants to talk about to do with pocket money" (or whatever is at issue) "so we can make sure we both know where we are, and we don't miss out anything important."

You will have to be honest here too, of course. I'm afraid that's the price you pay for training your children to be honest. But it's worth it to avoid that sinking feeling when they suddenly throw a fresh issue into the equation just as you thought you'd resolved it.

And what happens if, just supposing, you fail to take this precautionary step? It can happen, especially if you didn't realise until you were underway what a full scale negotiation this would turn out to be. The danger is that you will be pressured into making an instant response which you will regret later (obviously – that was their whole point in doing it). So don't let it happen. In fact, the solution lies in one of the rules of negotiating we'll cover later: agree to all or nothing. As you'll see, it will keep you out of the worst trouble here.

Never give free concessions

The technique: If the other side wants something from you, make it clear that you expect something in return. When they say, "We'll need a bigger discount – say, 15 percent", you don't simply agree. You make a trade-off: "We could only do that if you paid 30 percent up front." Don't yield concessions; trade them for concessions from the other side.

If your child states what they need and you say "OK, then" – even if it's only one of the variables and not the whole deal – you're not negotiating. You're giving in. You need to trade blow for blow (only metaphorically speaking, I hope) in order to clinch the outcome you want.

Do a deal on every point. When your son asks to go to the circus for his birthday party, say you can only manage that if everyone gets delivered straight home afterwards. When your daughter asks to stay up until 10 on Tuesday nights to watch a favourite programme, tell her she'll have to have her homework finished before bed regularly, and not leave it until the morning. When you ask your teenager to tidy his room and he offers to tidy the floor but leave his desk as it is, try saying, "You can leave the desk for now, but the leeches will have to go."

There are two reasons for trading concessions rather than giving them away. The first is that you are more likely to end up with what you need. It's the way to bring all those variables into play so that, although your daughter might now be staying up later, at least the lights are out at a sensible time, and her homework is getting done after school and not in a panicked rush at 7 o'clock in the morning.

The other reason for trading concessions is a psychological one (as with so many negotiating skills). You need to show your child that you're a tough negotiator, and that they needn't bother asking you to lower your requirements unless they're prepared to give something up too. This is even more important with children than it is with customers, colleagues and bosses, since you are likely to be involved in negotiations with your child for years to come (please accept my condolences), with no option of changing jobs or even being promoted into a new role.

Your best bet is to earn yourself a reputation as such a tough negotiator that unless your child is ready to compromise properly, they will choose not to negotiate with you at all but to pester their other parent instead. When that happens, you know you've got the skills of negotiating really licked.

Agree to all or nothing

The technique: You wouldn't sign a contract until all the points in it are agreed, and you shouldn't commit yourself to any part of a negotiation until all the points are agreed either. As soon as you give a definite yes to one point, you can no longer use it to bargain with. All your variables should slide up and down a kind of mental scale until they are all in balance – a little bit more money, but a better delivery time, and reasonable payment terms. Juggle them all, and play them off against each other, until they fit. If you lock off any one of them at a fixed, agreed point, you make the balancing act much harder – and sometimes impossible.

Negotiating is a bit like making a vinaigrette without a recipe. You put in a bit of oil, then a bit of vinegar, and sugar, salt, pepper, mustard and so on. You keep tasting it. If it's too sweet, you bump up the other ingredients to compensate. If it's not sharp enough, you add a little vinegar. If at any point you decide that you definitely aren't going to change the amount of oil in there, no matter what, you're going to be stumped if it's too vinegary. You've left yourself no room to manoeuvre. You need to be able to adjust all the ingredients until the dressing tastes just right.

So don't commit yourself to any of your child's requests until you can both agree to the whole deal. This is also a good insurance against the problems that arise if you don't get all their cards on the table before you begin, as we discussed earlier. As you discuss each issue in the deal you will, of course, reach a preliminary agreement on each one. But don't commit to it until they've all been discussed and a settlement reached on each. That way, you can bring an earlier issue back into play as a bargaining point if you need to.

So when the question of staying up until 10 o'clock on

Tuesdays seems settled, or the question of where to go for the party, or the level of pocket money, *don't* say "Right, that's agreed then." Instead, you should say something like: "Well, that sounds workable, so let's leave it for the moment and talk about the leeches…".

By the way, this is a mistake that many experienced managers and sales people make, so you'll be practising a valuable work skill on your child when you employ this technique with them. More to the point, you'll be keeping all your options open until you've got the deal you want.

Once you have agreed all the issues, balanced against each other in a way which satisfies everyone, summarise them before you finally commit – and get commitment from your child. If necessary, you can write it down between you so that you can see you're both happy with it. However you do it, make sure you're both clear what you've agreed: "So, you'll tidy the bedroom floor and the chairs, but you can do what you like with the desktop. You'll clear out all the rubbish from your room and put it out by the dustbin, and the leeches will be gone by the weekend. Every Saturday morning you can have an extra £2 pocket money if your bedroom is tidy – starting this Saturday. Are we both agreed?"

It's also a good idea to have some agreed indicator which signifies that the deal is done. Just as in business you shake on a deal and then sign, so too at home you need to be clear when the thing is settled, and negotiations are over. You might shake hands on it, or write it down and both sign the paper. Or you might simply know by the fact you're on speaking terms again. Whatever your system, make sure you have one so there are no further arguments on the subject.

Summary

However tough the negotiation is, never underrate the fact that your child is negotiating at all. Nobody takes part in a negotiation in the first place unless they have some underlying wish to deal with you, in preference to leaving things as they are or facing your wrath. Whether it is the Middle East peace process, or just you trying to encourage your seven year old to clean their teeth regularly, any negotiation is better than none.

Motivation skills: generate enthusiasm in your children

Children can be hugely enthusiastic and positive, and are capable of putting enormous effort into projects. They just have to feel motivated. You won't need to put any effort into motivating your teenage daughter to have her nose pierced, or your four year old to have a go on his new bicycle. However, motivation skills are essential if you want to get your children to do other things such as homework, or cleaning and tidying.

Managers need to motivate their staff just as you need to motivate your children. It can be a little tougher with children though. At work, your staff know that they have to put in some effort if they want to keep their jobs, so there is a level of self-motivation even if you need to build on it. At home, your children have no such incentive. You can't fire them, and they know it. Being your child is a job for life. So you sometimes find yourself faced with no motivation at all in your children, which you need to turn into sufficient enthusiasm to embark on a project and see it through.

As far as your role as manager is concerned, you need to keep firm control and be seen as a figure of authority and respect – rather than as a wimp – in order to get the performance you want to out of your team members. You need to use carrot rather than stick techniques to encourage your children to co-operate without undermining their confidence.

How can you get your children to want to do things they are not initially keen on? It might be cleaning out the rabbit hutch, getting their homework done, or going on holiday to somewhere you chose and they didn't. Or it might be a more long term issue: taking on extra chores, travelling to school on their own in future instead of getting a lift from you, or working harder at getting good grades in biology.

Whatever the issue, the selling skills we've already looked at will help. But even if you can sell an idea to your child in the first instance, you still need to keep them keen to pursue it to the end.

The truth about bribery

One of the best forms of motivation is bribery. It has a bad name among parents – it feels like cheating, but that's only because we associate it with a pathetic attempt at appeasement. It doesn't have to be. There's a world of difference between bribing a child to say yes after they've initially refused, and bribing them before you start. In other words, if you anticipate trouble, you can start out by saying "It's time to go shopping. Come on – if you're good I'll buy you an ice cream on the way home." It's not the same thing at all as begging your shrieking child, as they lie kicking and flailing on the floor of the supermarket, "Please be good, and I'll buy you an ice cream."

If you think about it, the first version – offering a bribe before they've done anything wrong – is only what managers do with their staff all the time: "If you're good, I'll give you a Christmas bonus." "If you handle this job well, you'll get more responsibility and a better job title next year." Some of these bribes are spelt out, and some are simply understood, but they are just as much bribes as an ice cream for being good at the shops is to your child.

So in future, we can stop calling these temptations bribes, and start calling them by the words we use at work: rewards, incentives, motivating factors. There. Now you don't have to feel guilty any more. You're not bribing your child, you're incentivising them. Just make sure you do it *before* they've misbehaved or failed to pull their weight.

Everyone is motivated by different things, as we'll see in more detail in a moment. But there are certain techniques you can use as a manager of either children or staff, which will help to motivate anyone. There are three key techniques:

- Show them how they fit into the big picture
- Set clear and realistic targets
- Involve them

Show them how they fit into the big picture

The technique: Let your staff see how their job fits in with the whole organisation. Show them what else goes on and explain how their role meshes with it. Let them see the results of their hard work: if they make wheel bearings for the cars you manufacture, let them drive one of the finished cars.

Your child is part of the whole family, and they need to understand their place in it. You might tell them that you can't take them out on Thursday; it may be their school holiday, but you've still got to go to work. But don't just leave it at that. Explain (helpfully, without lecturing) why the whole family benefits from you working. If you can, let them come to work with you for a morning and see what you do.

Why not swop jobs with your child for a day? (You might

need to modify this approach a little, especially for a small child.) Do it at a weekend when you don't have to go to work, or your boss might be a little surprised to see a smartly dressed six year old rolling up at the office and settling down on your chair, peeping up over the desk. Get your child to cook the dinner, wash the car, do the cleaning or whatever you do, while you do whatever it is they do at the weekend. You should have a pretty easy time of this (you're excused hanging around the shops pointlessly for hours with a large group of 14 year olds). Do their chores for them, though, before you put your feet up.

The object of the exercise is not to be able to say "See! I work my fingers to the bone all day while you do nothing." It is to help them see how what they do fits in (or otherwise) with what everyone else does. Make it as fun as you can. If you have more than one child, let them assume collective responsibility for all your chores, while you do all theirs.

Set clear and realistic targets

The technique: If you want people to improve their performance, you have to agree realistic targets for them to attain. If you don't, they don't know when they are doing well, which is a strong demotivator. So agree that their conversion rate of enquiries to sales should rise from 20 to 25 percent in the next three months, or that all brochures should be sent out within 24 hours of being requested.

How often have you said to your child, "You're going to have to clean the rabbit hutch out more often", or "Your bedroom's always such a mess: do something about it", or "Stop waking us up so early in the morning. Play for a bit by yourself first"?

We all do it, but we've only ourselves to blame when nothing seems to change. Of course they won't clean out the rabbit hutch more often – they haven't a clue what 'more often' means. Every day? Twice a week? And there's an added implication that you're not really bothered: if you were, you'd clarify what you want properly to make sure it really happened.

So if you want your child to improve their performance in some way, be specific. You may have to refer back to the chapter on negotiating to get them to agree to some of your targets (a four year old won't go along with playing quietly in their bedroom until 11 o'clock every morning without a fight), but make sure that you agree a specific figure.

Maybe you reckon they should tidy their bedroom every Saturday morning (although the amount of garbage that can collect in a teenager's bedroom in the space of seven days might seem like more than any human could shift in a morning. And the entire family supply of mugs and teaspoons will have vanished into the gloom by Tuesday.) Perhaps they should start their homework by 5.30 every evening. They could aim to clean out that rabbit hutch once a week, at the weekend, and top up the sawdust every Wednesday. And you could set an alarm for 8 o'clock for your four year old to let them know it's OK to wake you up now. (The next stage is to get them to do it by kissing you gently on the cheek instead of exploding in through the door and leaping on to the ~~trampoline~~ bed with a yell of "Wake up! NOW!")

Involve them

The technique: Always tell people what's going on in the organisation as far as you can. Ask for their ideas and suggestions when problems need solving. It should go without saying that you must be seen to be listening to the answers, too, even if you don't eventually act on them.

Involving people makes them feel they have a stake in what's going on, so they care more about it. And when it's a success, of course you must acknowledge their part in it.

It's easy to leave our children out of what's going on, and expect them to follow on blindly. With small children this is especially true. We tend to stick them in the car without even telling them where we're going – and then get annoyed if they complain when we get there. But it's not surprising really that they resent being dragged off to places without a by your leave – how would you feel? Older children tend to ask for the information, but it still makes them feel unimportant (to you) if they had to ask.

Of course, we generally leave our children uninformed because the matter at issue is nothing to do with them, or we think they wouldn't be interested. But this is missing the point. Obviously when you tell your 12 year old that the frumpy middle-aged woman who's just turned up is going to measure your bedroom chair for a new cover, you hardly expect them to get over excited about it. But at least you've demonstrated that they have a right to know what's going on. And until you tell them, who knows what they might be thinking? Perhaps they were imagining that she was a neighbour coming to complain about the loud music coming from their bedroom, or a travel company rep come to tell you you've won a family holiday abroad, or an animal welfare officer come to take away the poor, neglected rabbit.

Suppose you have a family problem. Say your children are getting old enough to have their own rooms but you're not sure how to fit them in. Do you move house? Divide a room in two? Build an extension? Whatever you do, involve the children. Explain the problem, and ask them what they think. They may have an idea you haven't thought of: "Why not convert the garage and I'll have a bedroom downstairs?" Whether you take their advice or not, if they've been involved in the discussion, they are far more likely to be motivated to go along with whatever solution you finally reach.

Find the right incentive

Those are the general guidelines for keeping people motivated, but of course you also need to find an incentive to encourage them to reach the targets you've set. And incentives can be very personal in terms of what works. Some people are highly motivated by money, while others go for security or status. You can motivate some small children simply by saying "It's a very grown up thing to do", while others will look blank and reply "But I'm not a grown-up."

There are several key rewards you can typically use to motivate people at work, and each of these can be adapted to suit your child – you'll know your child well enough to know which ones will work best. (Whichever they respond to, you'll probably find that the same factors will motivate them when they are adults and out in the working world.)

So here's a rundown of the key rewards managers use with their staff, and how to adapt them to give your child the incentive to do better. Of course, you can always employ more than one incentive to motivate your child. Some of these incentives and rewards can work either before or after the issue in question. For example, you might motivate a freedom loving child to do something by giving them freedom to do it their own way, or you might incentivise them by letting them know that if they co-operate, you will reward them with greater freedom of some other kind.

Money

The technique: You can offer your staff a raise, a bonus or a commission if they perform well, and for many people this is the most valuable reward you can give.

Clearly you don't need telling that many children respond extremely positively to the prospect of money, although the kind of financial incentive that will satisfy a five year old won't impress a 15 year old. But be inventive about how you offer money as an incentive – it doesn't have to be simply a question of handing over the cash if they do as you ask.

Certainly you can pay your children for doing certain tasks. Arguably it's only fair to pay them for doing a job which benefits you and not them – for example, washing your car for you. But you can also hold out the hope of an increase in pocket money after, say, three months if during that time they have consistently come home on time after evenings out, or done their turn at washing up without complaint (well, without excessive complaint – let's not make it too hard for them).

One of the best pocket money systems is to have two levels: a basic pocket money they get no matter what, plus an extra sum if they have done all their chores that week as well. You can then negotiate either of these to go up if they carry out extra chores or responsibilities.

You could even find a way to make the reward suit the situation. Suppose your teenage daughter doesn't want to clear out her wardrobe of all the old clothes she never wears any more. Offer her the price of a new outfit for doing the job. Every extra day it takes her to get round to doing it, you knock £10 off the budget.

Security

The technique: Some people are particularly resistant to change, and feel threatened by it. Money often represents security to these people, but so do other factors. Financially, they would prefer a small raise to the chance of a big commission – which they might not manage to earn. They want to know where they are. They might also be motivated by a good pension scheme, or by a permanent contract rather than a series of fixed term ones.

If you have a child who likes security and consistency, and is resistant to change, you can often motivate them by promising that in exchange for their co-operation you will make sure that certain things don't change. Suppose you're going to convert your garage so that your children can have separate bedrooms. Persuade the one who dislikes change that if they help with the decorating, you'll let them stay in the room they are in now. You can then find some other incentive – if you need it – to encourage the other one to move to the new room.

Never be afraid of using different incentives for each child. It might seem fair to treat all your children identically – and of course in some matters it is – but often it is far from fair. The same incentive has a different value for each child, and it's much fairer to offer parity of *value* to all your children than a superficially matching incentive.

Status

The technique: Promotion is a huge incentive to people who are motivated by status, but so is a better job title, a bigger office or a flashier company car. Or you could put them in charge of a prestigious new project.

When you look at your three or four year old, you can probably already tell whether they're going to grow up to be easily swayed by the promise of a fancier job title. By the time they are seven or eight, you'll certainly know. Introducing job titles within the family might not be practicable, and although your child would doubtless love their own 'company' car, you might not be so keen. But there is still almost limitless scope for conferring status as a reward or incentive.

The people your child will most want a high status with are their friends and peers. So this should be the source of your incentives. They will want the newest fashions, the latest bedtime, the flashiest CD player – whatever their friends hanker after. So these are the incentives to hold out as rewards for good performance. Again, if you can match the reward to the performance, better still. If their school shoes are clean every morning when they put them on, they can have a new pair of trainers at the end of term. That sort of thing.

One word of caution about offering status incentives: don't give a child higher status than their siblings. You can give them an important job such as being in charge of booking the family holiday (if that makes them feel important), but don't let them set the itinerary, or have powers to delegate tasks to brothers or sisters (they will find it hard to distinguish between delegating and issuing orders – together with threats if they see fit). You will drive a wedge between your children if you let them juggle status between them, as well as encouraging family rows. So stick to status symbols which are designed to impress their friends.

Recognition

The technique: Some people find their greatest reward in knowing that they have impressed you. They want to be appreciated. For these people, being praised and thanked for good work will mean more than a bonus or a smart new office (although giving them another reward as well as recognition often works even better than recognition alone).

Perhaps the easiest children of all to motivate are those who are eager for parental approval. If you have one of these, congratulations. They will often be happy to do something simply because you say "I'll be really pleased if you do it", or "You'd need to be pretty grown up to do this, but I reckon you might be able to."

This kind of motivation will only work over the long term if your child knows that you will recognise their achievement afterwards as well. You have to say "Well done!" If you often fail or forget to notice when they've done well, your claims that you will be really impressed or pleased when it's done will start to ring hollow. So follow through, and praise them when they succeed – it matters more to these children than to others (we'll look at how to give praise later on).

As these children grow older, it's a bit much to hope that recognition alone will motivate them every time. It may keep them going through the smaller tasks, like making you a cup of coffee at the end of the day, while their more money motivated brother or sister is asking "What's it worth?" But they're going to start wanting other rewards for bigger achievements, especially if they have siblings who are rewarded in other ways. It's no good saying "Well done, all of you. To show how grateful I am here's £20 for you… a new CD for you… and a big thank you for you."

Responsibility

The technique: In some cases, the best reward you can give is added responsibility. It can make someone feel important, or perhaps it just shows you trust them. Whatever their reason, putting someone in charge of a project, or giving them an extra responsibility, will encourage their long term commitment to you and to their job.

A lot of children like to feel grown up, and giving them more responsibility is often a great way to motivate them. If they feel important and trusted, they won't want to let you down. You can use this approach on very small children, by letting them play in the garden alone (while you watch neurotically through the window), if they promise to leave the sandpit tidy and not to open the hutch and let the rabbit out. Or tell them that if they're good going round the supermarket they can help you pack the groceries into bags at the checkout.

Older children will often respond well to being treated like adults and allowed to take responsibility for their own bedtime (so long as school grades don't suffer), or buying their own school bag if you just give them the money. If the rising phone bill is a problem – and it's not you who's been running it up – why not give your child their own phone and a fixed budget for calls and get the bills sent to them. They'll feel responsible and trusted, and they'll also have to pay any excess themselves.

The important thing to remember about responsibility is that it is very hard to take it away once you've given it. So if you are conferring a permanent responsibility, such as giving your child control of their own bedtime, you need them to prove they are capable of handling the responsibility before you give it if you possibly can. You could start by giving them control at weekends only, or you could have a probationary period for two or three weeks and a fixed review date at the end of it.

If they don't come up to scratch but they've clearly been trying, see if you can find a compromise settlement. Maybe you could give them a later bedtime for now, or give them control in the holidays. That way, they feel that although they didn't earn the full reward, at least you are recognising such achievement as they did manage.

Job satisfaction

The technique: No one is going to feel satisfied if they know they aren't doing their job well. So try to give people tasks they are well suited to, so they will be able to feel they've made a good job of it.

This incentive works for just about everyone, and is a very useful one when you're divvying up chores, especially if you have more than one child. It ties in with recognition, too: your child will need to hear you say "Well done. I knew if you were in charge of putting the rubbish out it would get done." (You don't have to add that it damn well ought to, seeing as they generate three quarters of the empty Coke cans, pizza boxes, biscuit wrappers and the rest of the rubbish.)

Some children are very active (they'd be good at changing the beds or clearing out the shed), some like to be outdoors (get them to mow the grass), some like things to be organised and tidy (they can load the dishwasher), some fancy themselves as being technically minded (put them in charge of changing lightbulbs – although not if they're only four)... you get the point. Give them a job they know they're good at, and then reinforce their own feeling by telling them how well they've done.

Challenge

The technique: People who enjoy a challenge are motivated by knowing that if they do a good job, you'll give them something else even tougher to get their teeth into. They relish the idea of being given training so that they'll be able to take on more difficult tasks in future.

A child who relishes a challenge will be happy to take on most responsibilities or tasks which they think will test their skills. So get them to work out for everyone how the new video recorder works, or make them responsible for drawing up the weekly shopping list. You can encourage small children of this type to learn new skills, such as getting themselves dressed in the morning, simply for the challenge of it.

The downside of motivating this kind of child is that they are often the most resistant to any chore which poses no challenge at all. Getting them to wash the dishes or tidy their room can be pretty difficult. So you might have to clean out the rabbit for them in exchange for them setting the video timer for you.

Freedom

The technique: Some workers – often the less orthodox types – particularly enjoy their own personal freedom. They are often motivated by being put in charge of their own time, being allowed to work from home or to work some kind of flexitime. Or perhaps they like tasks which give them plenty of opportunities to get out of the office more often.

If you have one of those children who is naturally resentful of authority, you can have trouble getting them to do anything. Even if you wield your authority with kindness and respect, they will resent it simply because it's there at all. The more control you can relinquish to them over their own lives, the happier they will be.

So don't ask this kind of child to clean out the rabbit hutch on a Saturday morning. Just say you want it done by Sunday night, and they can choose their own time over the weekend to do it. Put your small child's food on a plate in front of their own and let them help themselves, rather than present them with a *plate accompli* (if you'll forgive the pun). You'll have far fewer arguments over what they will and won't eat. The more freedom you allow them in carrying out the task, the more willing they will be to do it.

And when it comes to rewards, new freedoms – to walk to the shops on their own, or decide for themselves when they do their homework – are often the best incentives. You can even tie the job and the reward in together: you should have little difficulty persuading them to take sole responsibility for their own washing (on the condition that it still gets done, of course).

Praise employees

The technique: According to a recent survey of what gives people the most job satisfaction, praise came top of the ratings. If you want to motivate your staff, make sure you recognise good work and praise them for it. That doesn't simply mean giving them a pat on the back, however. If you want to get the best results from praising, you need to follow a few simple guidelines:

- Make the praise specific
- Talk about it
- Make it public
- Pass on praise from others

Children are deeply motivated by parental approval, and praising your children when they do well will encourage them to do well again to earn more praise. It is a carrot rather than a stick for getting good behaviour from your children, and one which will build their confidence and self-esteem at the same time. So apply the business guidelines to the way you praise your children, and motivate them as strongly as possible.

Make the praise specific

The technique: Don't simply say "Well done", or give your staff a hearty slap on the back. Tell them exactly what you're praising them for: show them you really noticed. For example, you might say "You did a terrific job of pulling together that presentation so quickly", or "Well done for calming that customer down. He was fuming and you handled him so well, he left smiling."

You can praise your children for big things or for small ones – the more the better. So you might say "Well done for getting such terrific grades in your exams, especially French and geography." But on a lesser point you might say to your three year old, "Wow! You mean you actually managed to fold your socks all by yourself? Well done!" Or "You were really good this evening about going to bed without a fuss." (OK, that's not likely to happen. But this is just hypothetical.)

Look for opportunities to praise your child. It may start to seem insincere if you praise them every five minutes for things which you both take for granted (such as your 16 year old managing to dress themselves. Mind you, getting *round* to putting their clothes on can be worthy of praise in some 16 year olds.) But find plenty of opportunities to praise genuine achievements, however small. Match your response to the importance of the achievement. You don't have to send a press release to the local paper just because your six year old remembered to clean her teeth at bedtime without being reminded. But you can still tell her you're impressed.

Talk about it

The technique: Show you are genuinely interested by talking about the work you are praising your team member for: "I still can't get over how impressed the customer was at the end of it – I could hardly take down their order fast enough. How on earth did you manage to get the powerpoint material ready so fast?"

Your child will feel really proud of themselves if you show real interest in their achievements. So talk about it. "You've managed to fold those socks really neatly, too. And you put them back in the right drawer." Another good idea is to ask them questions about it (it's amazing how much you can find to say about folding socks when you need to): "How could you tell you had got them both the right way round before you started folding them?" When it comes to the exam results, you could ask: "Which questions in the geography exam did you think you'd done best on?"

When you talk about the achievement you're praising, there is one important rule: never put a sting in the tail. If you finish with a negative point ("Shame about the biology result, though") you will undo all the good work you've just done. And next time you try to praise them, they'll just be waiting for the "But..." at the end. So don't even mention the fact that one of the folded socks in the pair is green and the other one has Thomas the Tank Engine all over it. It doesn't matter. They managed to fold them, and that's what you're talking about. Save any training in how to identify a *matching* pair for another time.

Make it public

The technique: Tell other people how well they did. Put it in the company newsletter if it's important enough. Mention them at a meeting when the boss is there. Write to the MD to draw attention to the excellent presentation they gave. Even when you're praising for a minor achievement, there's often an opportunity to mention it to a colleague or raise it at a team meeting. "Hey, Pat, have you seen how neatly Jim has reorganised this stationery cupboard?"

Telling someone else how well your child has done will mean a lot to them, especially if it's someone whose good opinion they value. So when your partner gets home, say "You'll never guess what Nick did this morning" – and make sure you say it in front of Nick. Or tell your child, "That's so good, I think I'll phone Granny right now and tell her you know how to fold your own socks. I bet she'll be impressed."

Pass on praise from others

The technique: Always tell your team members if someone else praises them to you. For example, "I'm told you gave a very slick presentation yesterday. When Jenny Smith called to place her order afterwards, she commented on how impressed she was." Or even a simple, "Fred was saying this morning how much easier it is to find things in that stationery cupboard since you sorted it out."

Passing on praise is not only praise from the other person, but constitutes praise from you too; you clearly took it on board and thought it worth passing on. So you give double the satisfaction by handing on praise in this way. It might be "Your French teacher told me she wasn't surprised you did so well in the exam, you've been doing really well all term, I gather." Or "Granny says that when you were over there at the weekend, you folded up her gloves beautifully for her all by yourself."

Summary

Motivating your staff is something you do naturally at work, because you know it's good for them and for you. And children who are, after all, only small grown-ups are motivated by the same factors. So make sure they feel like an important part of the family, and reward good behaviour in ways which really count for *them*. And if, like most parents, *you're* motivated by an easy and pleasant life, you should be very happy with the results.

5

Management skills: get the best from your kids

Managing children can be a lot like managing your team at work. Sure, kids can be difficult, uncompromising and manipulative, but then so can staff. All of them need to be motivated in order to get them to do what you want. They also need to be kept in check – sometimes even disciplined – when they step out of line.

Of course, you need to work doubly hard to manage your children well because, as I mentioned earlier, children have one great hold over you which your staff lack: you can't sack them. Imagine being saddled with the same team at work for 18 years, with no chance of them retiring, getting promoted, moving on or even, if their performance is truly dreadful, being given the boot. You'd really have to work at your management skills to make sure you all worked well and productively – and without throttling each other – for all that time. Well, now's your chance to practise... on your kids.

Children are all different, just as grown-up staff are, and you'll have different problems with each of them if you have more than one. Some are easy to handle, some are dreadful whingers, some are sulkers and others like to bend the rules. So at the end of this chapter you'll find a quickfire guide to managing some of the classic behaviour types you're most likely to come across in your children. You'll probably recognise most of them from colleagues, bosses or employees you've worked with too.

Give feedback

At work, what do you do when you find someone particularly difficult to work with? Maybe they are constantly negative, or perhaps they criticise a great deal. Or even, in the case of one person I used to work with, they are just too jolly – always singing and cracking jokes when you're trying to get through a huge pile of work.

What most of us do is to bottle the thing up. We don't know how to address it without confrontation, so we keep quiet and put up with it indefinitely. Or else, sooner or later, we snap. We let fly at them, and we either make them feel humiliated (which we didn't want) or they argue back and we're into a full scale row.

Wouldn't it be great if there was a better way? Well, there is, and it's called feedback. It works at the office and it works at home with the kids too. So whether they're forever leaving the milk out of the fridge, or they always whinge on long car journeys, or they never hang the towels back on the rail after their bath, you can resolve the whole thing without having to have an argument about it. Now doesn't that sound refreshing?

You may have learnt feedback skills at work, but in case you haven't, here's a summary of the key steps:

1. Find a quiet, unhurried opportunity to talk in private.
2. Plan what you want to say in advance so it comes out the right way.
3. Focus on how you feel, not what they do.

4 Listen while they have their say.
5 Be positive too: let them know you believe they can behave co-operatively.
6 Suggest a solution.
7 Be prepared to compromise.

We'll have a look at applying each of these techniques to your children in more detail.

Find a quiet, unhurried opportunity to talk in private

The technique: If you're going to offer criticism, however constructively, to a colleague or team member, you need to do it in a relaxing atmosphere to make it easier to keep the encounter pleasant. Never embarrasss them by giving feedback in front of other people.

If your child is just about to rush outside to ride their bike for a few minutes before that black raincloud bursts, it's not a good time to try to get their undivided and relaxed attention for a few minutes. Equally, you should not attempt to give feedback when they are engrossed in a television programme, doing their homework (you should be so lucky), have a group of friends round, or are in the middle of an argument with you about how to stack the dishwasher properly (or even whether it needs stacking properly).

Wait until you can catch them on their own (in the case of some teenagers you may have to wait several weeks for this), and when they are not rushing off to do something. Sit down – to prevent the feeling that you're about to disappear off somewhere – and have a quiet chat with them.

It's not a good idea to try to give feedback while your child is exhibiting the problem behaviour – it's much harder for you both to remain calm and objective. In other words, when they say, "But I hate doing the shopping. Why do I always have to come with you?", this is not the moment to reply "That reminds me, I wanted to talk to you about the problem of your whinginess."

Plan what you want to say in advance so it comes out the right way

The technique: The core of feedback – what makes it a successful technique – is the fact that it entails phrasing what you say carefully so as not to make the other person defensive. To be sure of getting this right, you need to decide ahead of time what you're going to say. The four key rules are:

- Don't exaggerate (with remarks such as "you're always complaining" – although in the case of a few people, children included, this is no exaggeration)
- Avoid judgements ("you're useless at putting up with anything you don't like")
- Don't use labels ("you're a whinger")
- Be ready to quote specific instances

Feedback-speak is about the only language which gives you a chance to tackle thorny topics with your child without it ending in tears (quite possibly your own). The system is designed to focus on the behaviour and not the child, so any criticism seems indirect. The first step in the process is to outline the problem to them as you see it. You do this by being fair and observing the first three rules above: no exaggerations, judgements or labels.

Very few people accept negative criticism readily, and I suspect your child is no exception. For criticism to be positive you have to be fair and objective from the start, and avoid any negative remarks. You will inevitably anger and demoralise your child if you imply that there is a constant problem when it is only in fact occasional. If you say, "You never help with anything" your child, who in fact probably does help from time to time, will wonder why they bother at all if you don't notice the good behaviour.

Avoiding judgements means addressing the problem from a neutral perspective without implying any moral standard to it. So don't tell your child that they are useless at this, or selfish about that. Simply state what they do without any moral or subjective comment. Of course, your child may well be selfish about not helping, but the aim of the exercise here is to solve the problem, not to vent your feelings. So keep your judgements to yourself, and simply say "you don't often help me to get meals ready or clear up afterwards." Telling them they are selfish may make you feel better, but is it honestly going to encourage them to be more helpful?

The third rule is to avoid labels. If you label people they start to feel they just are selfish or naughty or whatever label it is that you've applied to them. They can't change their nature, so they might as well give up. If they feel the label is unfair, they will equally wonder what is the point of trying to be helpful if you're just going to perceive them as being useless anyway. So don't tell them "You're a selfish boy," or "You're stupid," or "You never think of anyone but yourself". You need to approach them with the attitude that they are not a selfish child, they are a good child who has done a selfish thing. Far better to put it in a positive light and say "It's not like you at all. You're so helpful in other ways."

Positive labels are obviously far better for building a child's self-esteem and confidence, and giving them something to live up to. By all means tell a child they are friendly, clever, helpful or thoughtful. But with one proviso: only use accurate positive labels. Children get very undermined if you label them as clever but their school grades never live up to your assessment. Or if you label them as helpful when they're not, they'll see no reason to improve. But feel free to use accurate labels which are positive.

Finally, in terms of preparing what you're going to say, be ready with concrete examples. Your child is likely to respond initially by saying "When have I been whingy about going shopping?" or "But I helped you lay the table yesterday. When am I unhelpful?" You'd better have answers ready to these questions or the conversation could get very sticky. Your child is hardly going to settle for "Oh, I can't remember exactly. But I'm sure you're whingy quite often." And if you really can't come up with any examples, are you even sure your criticism is fair?

Focus on how you feel, not what they do

The technique: Don't make the person defensive by accusing them, saying "You do this," or "You make me feel…". Always start your sentences with "I feel…". So you might say "I feel frustrated when I want to look at the big picture and you want to discuss details." And explain why you feel this way: "I feel my time is being wasted on matters which you are capable enough to deal with on your own."

Children are not known for being humble when criticised, and levelling accusations at them will generate at least as strong a reaction as it does with people at work. If you say to your child: "You ruin my evenings by playing loud music when I'm trying to relax", you can't expect them to say "I'm so sorry. I never thought of that. How inconsiderate of me; it must be awful for you. I'll never put my CDs on after 7.30 in future." Actually, there is a possibility they'll say it, but only with a strong note of sarcasm in the voice.

So start with the words "I feel…" and see if you can't phrase the same thing in a less confrontational way. How about: "I feel frustrated when you play your music loudly in the evenings. It's my first chance to wind down after a long day, and I can't relax to loud music." There. That doesn't warrant an outburst in response; it's a perfectly balanced, reasonable comment, with no exaggeration, judgements or labels, and expressed from your own perspective. And you explained the problem briefly too.

Here's another example: "I feel taken for granted when I've prepared a meal for you and you don't offer to help clear up afterwards. It can take quite a lot of time and energy, and a few minutes input from you would be a big help."

Or how about: "I feel angry and worried when you go out without telling me. I'm responsible for you and concerned for your safety, and I'm left feeling helpless if I don't know where you are."

So always express the problem from your own perspective, and explain briefly why you see it as a problem.

Listen while they have their say

The technique: Don't go on about it. Once you've expressed your point of view, give the other person a chance to respond. Otherwise they'll start to get frustrated pretty quickly, and that will waste all the good work you've done so far.

Few things irritate children more than not being listened to. It's a child thing. Children are very conscious that their view often counts for less than anyone else's – or seems to – and the fastest way to wind a child up is to ignore, or appear to ignore, their feelings. If you do this, you've blown your delicate non-confrontational approach and you're back into full scale warfare.

So once you've outlined the issue, give them a chance to reply straight away. You'll get another chance to respond as soon as they've finished. But for the time being, listen. And show you're listening. Don't try to interrupt. Even if they've got a pathetic argument ("I have to play my music loudly or I can't hear it properly"), they still have a right to express their feeble attempt to wriggle out of the situation.

And they might have a really good point to make: "I didn't realise you wanted help at mealtimes. You've never asked for it." If this is true, you can probably resolve things easily if you accept their point of view. So instead of saying "Well I'm asking now!" or "I shouldn't have to ask!", you'll get a better result if you say, "That's a fair point, actually. How about I ask you now. Do you think you could help me out at mealtimes sometimes?" (Obviously you *shouldn't* have to ask. But equally obviously, with children you always *do* have to ask. It's just one of those things.)

Be positive too: let them know you believe they can behave co-operatively

The technique: Show you're being fair and friendly about the issue by pointing out when they have been co-operative: "I know you don't need to take a negative view of things. You were really positive despite the problems we had over the WPS contract last month."

This is another angle on not labelling, and a more positive one, too. If you are telling your child – however tactfully you put it – that they are a whinger, or a waste of space, there is a danger that they will conform to that image. So remind them that it doesn't have to be the real them. Give them a specific example: "You were great fun to be out with when we went shopping at the beginning of last week, so I know you can do it."

Suggest a solution

The technique: There's no point in complaining about something if you can't think of a better way of doing it. So don't enter into feedback unless you have come up with a solution to the problem. Your colleague or employee might volunteer a different solution (if the problem is that they're always negative they'll probably pick holes in yours anyway), but you should always have at least one to offer.

When it comes to finding a solution, you need to be realistic. And the most important thing to remember is that you can't change someone's personality, you can only change their behaviour. So if you try to turn your messy child into a tidy one, you will both become demoralised and frustrated when it doesn't happen. What you can do, however, is turn them into a messy child who hangs up the bathroom towels when they've finished using them, instead of leaving them on the floor. So tackle individual behaviours, not the whole personality. By the way, the bathroom towels won't be folded neatly and carefully over the towel rail – they'll still be a mess. But at least the mess will be on the rail instead of on the floor.

Before you begin feedback, you need to have thought through a reasonable, workable solution which takes into account your child's point of view as well as your own, and doesn't attempt to change their natural personality. Perhaps you could agree a rota for helping with meals, or maybe it could become your child's job to lay the table each meal.

Your small child who doesn't like shopping may need an incentive to stop whinging. To be frank, any child who doesn't like supermarket shopping clearly has a natural, sensible, healthy approach to life. Nevertheless, you probably don't enjoy it any more than they do, and being accompanied round the store by a small whinging object doubtless does nothing to improve the experience for you.

Maybe you could suggest that if they don't complain (at least, not beyond the necessary token objection any self-respecting child has to raise), you'll buy them a small treat at the end of the shopping trip. You'll have to stick to this firmly, of course. If you give in and buy a bar of chocolate or a magazine even when they have been whingy, you'll have wasted all this effort, and you'll be out of pocket buying treats too.

Be prepared to compromise

The technique: Listen to the other person's response to your solution, and be ready to compromise with them if necessary. They may have a valid point too, and it's only fair you should meet in the middle.

Don't expect to impose your prepared solution on your child without compromise. Your child might be prepared to turn down their loud music but not by as much as you'd like. Or perhaps they don't mind turning it off for an hour each evening if they can have it at full volume the rest of the time. So you may well find yourself into a negotiation at this point – but you know all about how to do that now, so you'll be fine.

Feedback is the best way to sort out minor criticisms and gripes with your child without it leading to rows and unpleasantness. As your children get older you can teach them how to do it consciously so that they can use feedback to minimise arguments with each other. And if – heaven forbid – they ever have a criticism of you, they can even use feedback to address that too.

Handle mistakes

The technique: The vast majority of accidents – especially in a well motivated team – are genuine mistakes. If the person who has made the mistake genuinely regrets it, there is no advantage to be gained by giving them a hard time about it. You will simply build up resentment.

So don't criticise people for making genuine mistakes. Make sure they understand how it happened and have learnt from it. Thank them for being honest enough to own up to it. That way, they will be happy to tell you next time they make a mistake.

Have you ever been ticked off for a mistake which you never saw coming and are sorry happened? It makes you feel really resentful. The fact that the person telling you off is doing so indicates that they don't think you're capable of feeling contrite enough without them telling you to. That doesn't say much for their opinion of you. And when it's not even true – you *were* already feeling sorry – it's just demoralising.

If you want to show your child that you respect them, one of the best ways is to accept their apology for a mistake without criticising them. Obviously this doesn't apply to repeated mistakes which they should have learnt to avoid by now – such as yet *another* coffee ring on your polished antique table – which may stray into the realms of the discipline interview, which we'll look at next.

However, you will be able to keep the number of discipline interviews down if you prevent mistakes from recurring. So when your child makes an avoidable mistake, it's not enough simply to smile indulgently and say "There, there. It wasn't your fault." You need to discuss it – without allocating blame.

The first thing to say is, "That's OK – I know you didn't mean that to happen." Then follow it up by checking they now understand the problem: "But do you understand now why putting my favourite wool jumper through the wash for me made it shrink?" Make sure they understand, and then ask, "How will you make sure it doesn't happen again?" (other than by binning the jumper which is now ruined for good). Be sure that they are aware of what they need to do to avoid a similar mistake in future. You could settle for, "I'll never, ever try to do your washing for you again", but ideally they'll understand that they mustn't put anything woollen through the washing machine, and that if they are in doubt they should ask first.

Discipline

No good manager likes to conduct a discipline interview, and parents don't enjoy having to discipline their children either. But whether you're dealing with a wayward employee or a wayward child, it will always be easier and more effective if you approach the whole thing in a calm, matter of fact, pragmatic manner. Emotions get in the way of successful disciplining. And while you may have only partial control over the other person's emotions, you can certainly keep on top of your own.

The first step, before you ever conduct the interview, is to check your facts. And there are two basic areas to check:

- Their performance
- The standard for the job

Their performance

It's humiliating for you, and unpleasant for the other person, if you try to discipline them for something they haven't done. When you accuse your employee of being late three times last week, only to discover they cleared it with their supervisor first, you're going to feel pretty silly. Equally, if you accuse your child of stealing money from your wallet and they deny it, you'll be at an instant stalemate unless you've checked what actually happened.

So you need to establish what happened, and be able to prove it if there's any chance they'll deny it. Do this in advance and you'll be confident of your facts. What's more, they'll pretty soon learn that there's no point denying these things because you're bound to have evidence – you always do.

The standard for the job

You also need to be clear about what your employee or child thinks is expected of them. If you've never made it clear what time your employee was supposed to turn up in the morning, you can't very well tell them they're late, just because *you've* decided they should be in by 9.30. And perhaps your child thought it was OK to take money from your wallet so long as it was for a legitimate reason. Perhaps it was their school lunch money for the week, or maybe you told them a couple of weeks ago that you'd pay for them to go swimming. Unless the other person knew that what they were doing was wrong or not up to standard, you shouldn't be disciplining them at all. You should simply be having a chat to agree standards for the future.

Having got your facts straight on these two areas – their performance and the standard expected – the purpose of disciplining is simple. You need to close the gap between the two. Their performance hasn't reached the standard for the job, and you need to do three things in your discipline interview:

1. Agree with the other person that there is a gap ("OK, yes, I know. I'm not allowed to eat the food you've bought in for your dinner party tonight").
2. Establish why there is a gap ("I was really hungry and the individual salmon terrines were right there, and I couldn't be bothered to make a sandwich instead").
3. Find a way to close the gap ("Alright. I'll go out to the supermarket right now and buy you a replacement with my own money, and I won't do it again").

One of the key rules about disciplining someone for a persistent problem is to catch it early. If they're late for work once, you might overlook it. As soon as it happens again, deal with it. Don't wait until it has happened four or five times. There are two reasons for this.

Firstly, it makes the interview far easier. You're only dealing with a very minor problem at this stage, so there's no need for anyone to get heated or upset. You're simply tweaking their performance slightly, not completely overhauling it. It's far easier to get your child to pay back the money they borrowed from you when it's only £5, than to wait until they've built up a debt of £500.

And secondly, the very fact that you haven't said anything until now will have implied that you were happy with the way they were performing. If your employee has turned up for work at 10 o'clock most days for the last three months, they will probably be surprised and put out when you suddenly announce that it's a disciplinary matter. They had probably concluded by now that it was perfectly acceptable. Equally, if you tell your 12 year old that they have to go to bed at the prescribed bedtime, they are likely to resist you strongly if they've been ignoring their bedtime since they were seven and getting away with it.

So, having established your facts, and identified the process (agree the gap, establish the reasons for it, and find a way to close it), it's time to conduct the interview itself. Having laid the groundwork, this should be pretty straightforward so long as you observe the groundrules.

Conduct effective interviews

The technique: We've already seen that you need to be relaxed and calm to conduct the interview. If you're fuming about the fact that your employee has taken a crucial decision without any reference to you, for example, wait until you've calmed down before you talk to them about it. If *they* become emotional and tearful, be sympathetic but don't allow it to put you off or change your standards. Then follow the five rules of engagement:

1 Get them to talk
2 Stick to the facts
3 Focus on the problem, not the person
4 Maintain confidentiality
5 Be consistent

Get them to talk

The technique: You need to establish the reasons for the gap between the standard for the job and their actual performance. But if you want your employee's co-operation, this is far better coming from them. So don't weigh in with your own opinion; ask them why they haven't met the agreed standard. Encourage them to open up and talk about it by asking them open questions (we covered this earlier), such as "What was the reason you took this decision without discussing it first?"

Get your child to talk about what happened, rather than sulking silently. Ask them questions beginning "Why…?", "How…?", "In what way…?" and so on. For example, "How come you left the bathroom for half an hour after you'd turned the bath taps full on?"

Stick to the facts

The technique: Your team member may well try to wriggle or get defensive by coming up with all sorts of excuses for their behaviour. You can get round this simply by coming back to the facts. "But you did take the decision yourself even though I was around to ask, didn't you?"

Any self-respecting child is going to try to come up with an excuse. "I just went to answer the phone", or "I fell asleep", or "I thought I'd forgotten to put the plug in."

Just keep bringing them back to the facts, gently but firmly. "Nevertheless, the living room was flooded and the computer reacted by blowing up. And the reason was that you left the bath taps running for half an hour, wasn't it?"

Focus on the problem, not the person

The technique: If you want to keep the mood relaxed and adult, don't focus on the employee's personality. Don't tell them "You're arrogant", or "Your problem is that you think you can do everything yourself". That is *not* the problem. The problem is that a decision was taken without reference to you when you should have been asked to OK it.

Children are great at saying "Well, I was only...", or "I just thought...". Don't jump down their throats with "No you didn't, you never think. That's your problem." This breaks all the rules we've established in the past (don't exaggerate, don't label, and several others – including your own promise to yourself that you'd never sound like your mother). More to the point, it doesn't work. It makes them defensive and understandably emotional, which gets in the way of a successful outcome to your discipline interview.

So never mind telling them that they're always absent-minded, or thoughtless, or in a dream. Maybe they are. But they can't change the way they are, so there's no point trying to make them (anyway, it's what you love them for, isn't it? Just remind yourself of that while you're cleaning up the flood downstairs, and earning the money to get the computer fixed). Just concentrate on the problem, which is that the house was flooded because the bath taps were left on, not that you have an irresponsible child.

Maintain confidentiality

The technique: Never pass on to anyone else any details of what was said at a discipline interview. You'll never get anyone to talk freely in such an interview again if you breach confidentiality, and you'll upset them deeply. Even if the discipline resulted from a complaint by someone else, that person needs to know only that the matter has been dealt with. Your employee, on the other hand, can say what they like to anyone about it.

It's important for your child to feel that once the problem is resolved and the interview is over, the matter is forgotten (given that any lessons have been learnt – such as turn the taps off before you leave the room). This means they aren't left with a sinking feeling, or a sense that there is trouble in the air. One of the most important ways of doing this is to keep the matter properly closed once it's sorted out.

So don't go round telling people what happened, and what was said. If their best friend's mother says "I hear you flooded the house the other day. And you claimed you'd fallen asleep!" they will think twice before they open up to you about anything else.

Yes, I know that it's impossible not to tell close family when your four year old cutely explains that she only took the money from your wallet "to leave it out for Santa Claus, because nobody pays him for working so hard." But if there's any chance your child will mind you passing on what they've said, or what action they've agreed to take, at least restrict yourself to telling people who will keep it to themselves. And if you possibly can, resist even that.

Be consistent

The technique: Make sure that you apply the same rules to everyone.

If you come down hard on John for being late twice when you gave Phil only a mild telling off for being late half a dozen times, you'll build up resentment very quickly, along with accusations of favouritism.

If you have more than one child, you need to make sure you discipline and punish them all equally for comparable offences. This means remembering what punishments you have meted out in the past, because you know perfectly well that your children will remember them with stunning accuracy. "But you made him go to bed half an hour early for a week when he did it, and now you're making me go to bed an hour early for four nights. So you're punishing me for half an hour more than him." You could try arguing that it's all down to inflation, but you'd be better off getting it right in the first place. Keep a notebook or a diary if you need to.

Once you've agreed the action you're both going to take to close the gap between standards and performance, you need to make sure it happens. This includes making it clear what will happen if the problem recurs. Don't leave it open to speculation. Tell your child, "If it happens again, you won't be allowed to run the bath for yourself", or "You'll be banned from using the bath for a month" (although I don't recommend this particular one unless you also have shower). Make sure they know exactly where they stand, and there's much less chance that they will need disciplining again. Well, at least not for that particular offence.

Deal with problem people

We like to think that our children will grow up to be sensible, rational adults. But experience shows us that a lot of the grown-ups we know haven't managed it. Many of our colleagues, bosses or staff exhibit traits which we fondly hope our children will have outgrown long before they are released into the community.

However, the good news is that if you know how to cope with manipulators, sulkers and the like at work, you can also handle them at home. So if your son blames his big sister for everything, or your daughter goes into deep sulks, you can apply the same techniques to them as you do to a team member who always passes the buck, or a colleague who sulks at the slightest excuse.

The thing to remember with these people – of whatever generation – is that you cannot change their innate personalities, and you shouldn't try. A daydreamer will always be a daydreamer. Your task is to find a way of coping with the daydreaming, or putting it on hold when things need to be given fuller concentration.

People who never listen

The technique: The problem with these people is that they often fail to do things, or do them wrong, and then claim you never asked them to do the job, or didn't mention that they'd have to check with accounts first. The solution is to get them to repeat instructions back to you. If you think they're repeating them parrot fashion, without actually taking them in, ask open questions about the task: "How do you think we should deal with visual aids for the presentation?"

How often have you heard your child excuse themselves for not doing something by saying, "You never asked me to!" Some children genuinely believe this is true; they're not trying to be naughty. They really didn't hear you. So if you need them to hear an instruction or a piece of information ("Great Auntie Marjorie's coming to tea, so *watch your language*"), follow it by making eye contact (hold their face if necessary) and saying, "I want to be sure I've made this clear. Could you repeat it back to me?"

If they reply in a fashion which gives you the least suspicion that they haven't actually taken it in, ask them an open question: "Which words do you particularly need to avoid when Great Auntie Marjorie is here?"

Daydreamers

The technique: Daydreamers tend to get distracted in the middle of tasks, and make mistakes or get sidetracked. Anything they find boring is especially likely to send them off into their dream world. So keep them stimulated and interested, and set them tasks to do with other people – a colleague will keep them wide awake and focused on the job.

Your child is always going to daydream if they're bored. And often, it's a good quality. They probably whinge less because they can withdraw into a world which is always interesting, and they most probably have a wonderful imagination. However, imagination won't get the bedroom tidied.

Forget trying to give your child any boring, monotonous jobs to do unless they can either dream as they do them (like drying the dishes), or you don't mind how many weeks elapse before the task is complete. Give them interesting tasks.

If boring tasks need doing (and let's face it, the chores at the top of the list always seem boring) do them together, so you can keep them alert. Or, if you have more than one child, get them to share two tasks between them, rather than doing one each. This may be the greater of two evils if they're inclined to fight, but for some siblings it works very well.

Manipulators

The technique: The key to understanding manipulators is to recognise that they don't manipulate without a reason. They always have a hidden motive. They will never give you enough evidence to prove they're manipulating, so an open challenge will be denied. But you can work out why they're doing it if you're clever, and then tackle the root cause. So if Jenny is trying to make Dave look bad, maybe it's because she wants the promotion when Phil leaves, and she's worried you'll promote Dave instead. Simply talk to her and say, "I get the feeling that you might be interested in Phil's job when it comes up. Is that right?" This gives her the chance to be open rather than underhand with you. She'll go for it, because it gives her a better chance of getting what she wants.

You know it was Harriet who planted your wallet in Max's bed to get him into trouble. But you can't prove it. It's OK, you don't need to. Just work out why Harriet wants to get Max into trouble. Is she jealous of him? Is she paying him back for getting her into trouble yesterday? Whatever the reason, sit Harriet down and talk to her about it. If you reckon she's trying to pay Max back, say, "I sense that you're still angry with Max for filling your boots with yoghurt yesterday?"

Perhaps Harriet feels that Max wasn't sufficiently punished, or that everyone thinks his practical jokes are funny and doesn't give her enough sympathy. You can't backdate Max's punishment, but you could offer to talk to him again, or assure her that any future yoghurt incidents will incur more serious punishments (and tell Max too). Whatever you agree, you have removed the need for any manipulative behaviour. Oh, and the wallet in the bed never needs to be mentioned at all.

Buck-passers

The technique: It's always someone else's fault. "Sorry I didn't get the filing on your desk cleared by Monday, but Kieran suddenly dumped a load of work on my desk on Thursday." You have to make it absolutely clear to these people exactly what needs to be done, and make it clear that if there's a problem they must tell you straight away. If they come to you on Thursday complaining that the job won't be done on time, just use the stuck record technique: "The extra work from Kieran obviously makes it harder, but I still need all the filing cleared by Monday." If they continue to protest, ask them "What are you going to do about Kieran's work to make sure my filing is still cleared by Monday?"

The child who blames school, a brother or sister, a parent or a friend for every failure to deliver the goods, needs to learn that it is their responsibility to cope with the problems all these other people seem to throw at them. You need to make it clear that they still have to dry the dishes after dinner, or whatever it is. Be specific about the job: "I want them all dried, and I want it done straight after the meal, not later in the evening."

If they say "Sarah's coming over and she'll be here by 7.30, so I won't have time", simply reiterate the task. "I can see that's difficult, but you still need to dry the dishes straight after dinner." Keep persisting. Suppose the next excuse is, "Sarah's already bought tickets for a movie and it starts at 7.45 so I shan't have time," just keep going. Make it clear that it is their responsibility to cope with these problems and still get the job done. Ask, "How are you going to arrange it so that the dishes still get done straight away?"

In this case the ultimate sanction, of course, is that they will have to miss the movie. Once they learn that you won't back down, they will have to learn to cope with Sarah or whoever else it may be, and fulfil their responsibilities no matter what.

Whingers

The technique: Whingers are generally a bit of a pain to have on your team. On the other hand, they are often keeping everyone else quiet. The fact that they are guaranteed to moan means that everyone else feels they don't have to. The more you can involve whingers in what's going on, the less they will whinge. If they helped to formulate a decision, they can't very well complain about it. The other specific technique you can use is to ask them *before* they start to whinge if they need any help. If they say yes, you can provide it. If they say no, it's harder for them to complain later.

For many parents, the classic whinger is the one who complains about long car journeys (they usually start whinging before they've even got in the car). Maybe you can involve them in the decision to make the journey. Ask them if they'd like to go on holiday to the seaside, instead of just booking it yourself without consulting. Remind them about the long journey. When it comes to it, at least they'll realise they volunteered for it.

The day or morning before the journey, ask them if they need anything to keep them amused. Be prepared to supply magazines or games or packets of crisps if they ask (though perhaps you might draw the line at going out and buying them a laptop). Not only should this do the trick, but they will feel you sympathise with their low boredom level on long journeys, rather than simply being irritated by it.

Sulkers

The technique: Sulking is designed to make you feel guilty once you realise how deeply upset the sulker is. If you *are* guilty, you should apologise, which is what they want. So once you've apologised (sincerely and appropriately), they'll stop sulking. However, you may not feel guilty in the least. In this case, reassure yourself that the sulker has really had a fair chance to have their say. A lot of us sulk if we feel we're not being taken seriously, so make sure this isn't the case (and if it is, hear them out). If you're clear on this score too, don't capitulate. If you ever give in to a sulker – and let them find out it works – they'll try it every time they're unhappy. Just ignore them, and say "We'll discuss it later." Don't make things worse by sulking or fuming back. Pretend everything's normal, and they'll give up when they find sulking doesn't work.

A sulky child can bring a heavy atmosphere over the whole household. On the other hand, the ones who don't sulk probably throw tantrums, which is arguably worse. At least with a sulker you can get on with your life and ignore them.

But stick to your guns. If you've said they can't have a motorbike, they can't have a motorbike. Let them see that sulking isn't going to help one jot. And then behave as if they aren't sulking anyway. It's a slow business, but over the months and years you can train a child out of sulking this way (well, most of the time). If you give in to it, however, they will get worse – that's probably what your sulky colleague's parents did.

Prima donnas

The technique: These are the ones who never sulk – they throw a tantrum instead. "I can't believe you let someone else handle that contract! After all the work I'd put into it! For crying out loud…" And like sulkers, they do it because it works. So don't give in to it. Take the wind right out of their sails by leaving the room. "I'm just going to get myself a coffee. I'll talk to you about this later." You should also (if you are trapped in the room with them) refuse to get heated and emotional in response. Simply be cool, rational and objective.

The standard approach with a prima donna of a child should

be to ignore them completely. Behave as if they weren't there. It will drive them mad this time, but in the long term it will show them that their method doesn't work. Leave the room; without an audience, they're lost. If they follow you, you can either ignore them or send them to their room.

If you send them to their room, however, don't show any sign of being emotional yourself (because that's what they want – to know they're getting to you). Just smile and say "Off you go to your room; you're being a bit too noisy to stay down here. You can come down when you're calm, and if you want me to I'll explain again why you can't have a motorbike. See you in a bit. Bye."

Give them all the time they want to talk, discuss and reason when they're calm, but refuse to talk as soon as they become emotional. It won't take them long to realise which behaviour is in their best interests.

Summary

Coping with children can seem like running a department or a small organisation, which is why many of the techniques are the same. And although, in a family, you can't sack your staff – or even take a holiday without them tagging along too – you can train them more easily than you can adults whose behaviour patterns have been set for years. When times get tough, console yourself with the thought that some manager, somewhere, someday, is going to consider your child the perfect employee once they've grown up – thanks to you. (Whoever that manager is, they're probably only 11 years old right now, and quite possibly in the middle of a tantrum as you read this.)

Teamwork skills: show your children how to get along together

One of the most frustrating parts of being a parent – if you have more than one child – is the constant rows and the endless sniping and tale-telling that can go on between children. It's a shame, because you want them all to be friends. And the older they get, the more you want them to look out for each other and be supportive when things are tough. If you think about it, brothers and sisters probably know each other for longer than they know anyone else in their lives. And even when you're not there for them any more, you'd like to know that they're there for each other.

That's why teamwork skills are so useful in bringing up a family. Not only do they minimise the rows (I'm afraid I'd be lying if I claimed they remove them altogether), but they also help bond your children into a strong and supportive unit. The aim is to have a family which functions as an effective team, with the children as a kind of sub-team within it.

There are several management techniques which have a long track record of effectiveness in helping to pull together a group of people into a team, even when the department includes people from a wide range of backgrounds and ages.

So they should be a doddle with your kids, who are from the same background, and relatively close in age. You simply have to know how to motivate your children to care about the team unit – the family – so that they are not focused solely on themselves.

It's also worth bearing in mind another team building principle: nothing unites people better than a common enemy. You may have noticed how a work team which is so disparate or rife with friction that it hardly merits the title 'team', will suddenly pull together in the face of a strong competitor likely to steal a contract from them, or when worried that the board is going to decide to base them 20 miles away at a different branch office.

In the case of your children, the most promising common enemy is you. This is not to say that you should go out of your way to behave like an enemy, but every so often your children will cast you that way because you said no to their having a new bike, or you shouted at one of them over dinner when they hadn't done anything wrong – they simply wanted to dunk their apple pie in the leftover gravy. And then, of course, they have a moan to each other about you.

Don't discourage this. Their negative attitude to you will soon blow over, and in the meantime they are building stronger ties with each other as they agree about how cruel and inhuman you are in a way in which they have never agreed about which channel to watch, or where to go for a day out. Shared bedrooms are a great way to encourage your children to bitch about you together, along with sitting them next to each other in the back seat of the car (where they can whisper irritatingly just out of your earshot), or simply leaving them alone in a room together after you've refused a request or got angry with one of them.

Foster team spirit

The good news is that there are plenty of principles you can apply to family life to encourage your children to feel like part of a team – and a team that they want to belong to. So here are the key guidelines for building a great team at home.

Encourage your team members to support each other

The technique: If one member of your team needs help or advice, you don't have to be the one to provide it yourself. Suggest they ask a fellow team member – or you could ask them. This helps the team form good working relationships between themselves that don't have to incorporate you every time. Equally, if one member of the team has a really urgent task to complete, get all available hands on deck to get it done.

If one of your children needs help with their maths homework, why not ask their older brother or sister to help instead of doing it yourself? It will make them feel important, and will get the pair of them working together. Not to mention leaving you more time to get on with other things. It never hurts to get your children to help each other, whether it's washing each other's backs in the bath or learning to put on make-up.

If you want to help construct solid, equal relationships in the family, however, even the youngest child has to be able to give support as well as receive it. They can certainly help out with chores (although they may not see it that way), and they may well be able to provide information that the others want: "Why not go and ask Jamie about that – he's the expert on leeches."

If you're looking for opportunities to encourage support between your kids, you should find that youngest children develop particular skills quite early on. A six year old may well have a talent for setting the timer on the video, and can be called on to do it for an older brother or sister. Or they may know more than anyone else in the family about horses or trains. Don't miss a chance to refer an older sibling to them for information rather than supplying it yourself.

When one of your children has an urgent or difficult job to do, call everyone who is free together to help. If you make this fun, they will want to join in. Maybe your teenager is packing to go on a school trip and is running late – you can get everyone running round the house finding spare socks and tracking down a sponge bag. Or perhaps your 10 year old is having trouble assembling their new go-kart and needs a hand. And then there are family crises to involve everyone in too, such as bailing out the garage when it floods after a heavy storm. If you enjoy it instead of panicking or barking orders, you children will enjoy it too – and they'll learn that things go far more smoothly when they all pull together.

You can't call all hands on deck five times a day, or everyone will get fed up with the workload. But every few weeks it's a great team activity.

Put different people in charge of different projects

The technique: You can encourage mutual respect between your team members by giving everyone some responsibility. It will help them to realise that people are in charge of tasks, not simply in charge of other people for the sake of it. Having put someone in charge of a project, you must back them up publicly, and do things their way along with everyone else. If there are any problems, you should sort them out with the person behind closed doors.

This is a great technique to use with children – they really appreciate the responsibility. It may seem unfair to put one child in charge of something over the others, but it works so long as you bear in mind two important guidelines:

- Don't put children directly in charge of each other – only in charge of the task itself
- Choose the responsibilities carefully – make sure they won't lead to major conflict

For example, you could put one child in charge of the shopping list – making sure that if anyone uses up the last of something, it gets written down. And checking there's always a shopping list pad with a pen next to it. This is a responsibility that involves everyone, but doesn't put anyone in charge of anyone else. Your child can, however, introduce a better system and ask everyone to follow it. The responsibilities you choose have to concern everyone, or they have no impact on your objective to foster team spirit. It's fine if one of your children is detailed to take the vegetable peelings out to the compost heap every day, but it isn't going to impinge on their siblings.

If you want some more suitable responsibilities, organising practically anything – and keeping it organised – generally works well: sorting out the video cupboard, keeping the larder stocked with snack foods, or organising the travel arrangements to and from school (best not to leave this to your five year old, mind). As we saw in the last chapter, give children tasks they are good at and they'll enjoy them more.

If you're worried your children will set unreasonable standards and then row with the others when they don't stick to them ("You've got to colour code every video, as soon as you record it, with one of these eight dots according to this code I've written down. If you don't, I'll wipe your video"), you can always stipulate that any new system should be cleared with you first.

Train the team collectively

The technique: Group training sessions bring people together. So if they all need to know something, tell them all at once.

"Right, kids. This is how the new washing machine works." It's easier to tell everyone at the same time – you only have to go through it once. And they all feel equally involved. What's more, they can giggle together when you get it wrong and flood the kitchen.

Reward the team as a whole

The technique: If the team works well together, reward them collectively rather than rewarding each person individually. This reinforces the importance of the collective contribution everyone is making. Give everyone an equal share in the reward, whatever their contribution.

If your children work well as a team, don't give them each £5, or an individual treat. Buy ice creams all round, or take everyone out for a trip or a special meal. Or maybe redecorate a shared bedroom or playroom, or buy the popcorn maker they all want.

It's a good idea to create team activities which are fun – fun is a huge motivating factor – and then reward achievement. For example, you could time how long it takes for you all to clear up after a meal. One stacks the dishwasher, one washes the pans, one clears and wipes the table, and so on. Every time you beat your previous record, everyone shares a reward (better check first that those pans really are clean).

Avoid obvious areas of friction

The technique: Don't throw people into close working relationships together if you know they're going to rub each other up the wrong way. You can't force people to get along if they just aren't made that way. When you do have to ask them to work together, try to add a third person who can help to keep the peace.

If you've been following all the guidelines in this book, it's unlikely that you will have two children who really dislike each other. However, you probably will have two children who irritate each other in certain respects. Most parents do. When this happens, don't put them together for tasks which will obviously bring these problems to the fore.

Suppose one of your teenage children is careful and methodical, while another is slapdash and rushes everything. If you ask the two of them to redecorate their bedroom together, you're asking for trouble. Equally, it wouldn't be a good idea to get them to assemble the flat-packed wardrobe together. Either get a different child to do each job, or join in yourself and keep the peace – encourage the methodical one to do the gloss work on the windows while the slapdash one does the emulsion on the walls. Meanwhile, you can try to put together the wardrobe and give them both a shared laugh at your expense.

Discourage division within the team

The technique: The unity of the team is crucial, and more important than any petty disagreements within it. So don't encourage your team members to make complaints against each other, or come running to you when a colleague has put their nose out of joint. Make it clear that you prefer them to sort out their differences by themselves.

As soon as you take sides – however justified – you are necessarily splitting the team. This is clearly not something you want, so you need to avoid taking sides in the first place. Obviously if one of your children hospitalises the other, you're going to have to express a view. But keep clear of everyday niggles of the "I was sitting there" variety. Obviously you'll have to teach very young children to deal with these squabbles before you can take a back seat, but as they get older they should be able to handle them alone.

The other thing to discourage firmly is tale-telling. It is guaranteed to divide the team if your kids think they can get away with it. And what a great way to get a brother or sister into trouble (to pay them back for pinching their seat). The only way to prevent this divisive behaviour is to ensure it doesn't work. So when your ten year old daughter says, "Mark didn't do his homework last night, and then he told the teacher he'd left it at home", your response should be "Well, he shouldn't have done that, but you shouldn't be telling tales either."

To complete the effect, you now have to resist saying anything to Mark on the subject. This way, his younger sister has had a minor ticking off, and Mark has had none. It won't take long for it to sink in that telling tales gets you nowhere, and your children should learn that you value their loyalty to each other higher than any petty information they may pass on. So they certainly won't snitch on each other if they are seeking your approval.

Obviously you may occasionally have to intervene – for example, if one of your kids tells you that their five year old sister is smoking 10 a day – but almost every time you're better off letting it pass. If the other child knows they've been snitched on you may feel you have to say something or you'll appear to condone the behaviour. In that case don't tick them off, or you'll encourage the tale-teller, but simply say (with a smile – but so they know you mean it): "You got away with it this time. But don't let *me* catch you doing it."

Exploit each team member's strengths

The technique: The better the team performs as a whole, the more motivated its members will be. They will see that they could not have achieved nearly so much alone, but that their own contribution has been crucial. So give everyone the chance to shine for the benefit of the whole team. Give people tasks which exploit their strengths.

We've touched on this before, but not in the context of building team spirit. However, it is important to allocate tasks in team activities according to each child's strengths. That way, at the end of the project, they will all see and value each other's input, and they'll realise that everyone else appreciates their contribution.

Maybe it's the last minute rush before you go off on holiday. So get your methodical child to do the packing, while the hyperactive one cycles down to the shops for a picnic to eat on the train. Meanwhile, the organised one can collect up extra items that might have been forgotten to give to their sibling who is packing – first aid kit, sunblock and so on. And you can have a rest – after you've sorted out the clean washing, tidied the house, checked the windows are all locked, written the note for the milkman, taken the cat to the cattery…

Just one thing to watch out for here: if you have two children with a similar strength, don't always give the jobs which need this quality to the same child. You may think Tom is pretty organised but Sophie is the really organised one. But if you always say "Sophie, you can do this – you're always so good at organising things", Tom is going to feel pretty unappreciated. You may value the fact that he's the best problem-solver, but he will see only that you don't appreciate his organisational abilities. So make sure none of your kids is harbouring a secret feeling that they are being overlooked.

Communicate with your team

The way you communicate with your children is a big part of helping them feel like a unit. If you treat them as a team, they will behave like a team. There are two key techniques for achieving this:

- Involve them in what's going on
- Brief them as a team

Involve them in what's going on

The technique: You can't expect your team to feel like part of a strong unit if they have no input into what that unit does or how it does it. So involve your team members in decisions which will affect them: "Our workload is going to increase next month once the new system comes on line. How are we going to cope with it?" You can still take the final decision, but they will feel part of the process.

One of the best ways to build up a strong family identity is to give your children a say in what goes on. Not only will they feel more motivated to co-operate in it having been involved in the decision (even if it isn't the one they voted for), but they will also see that everyone else's opinion is important as well as their own. There are certainly times when you have to inform your children what's going on without their input ("Great Auntie Marjorie's coming to stay for a fortnight"), but more often you can consult them before you make your final decision: "It's time to get rid of our car and get a new one. What do you all reckon we need from the family car – what features should it have?"

You'll find that when you give children this kind of opportunity, they live up to it admirably. They might want a Ferrari or a Thunderbird, but they know perfectly well they're not going to get it. And they may have sensible suggestions to make about the amount of space it should have, or a valid request for a sunroof. Even if they suggest nothing you haven't thought of already, they will still feel they have a stake in the final decision. Who knows, they may even feel more inclined to keep it tidy (sorry… got a bit carried away there…).

Consult your children in a group – family mealtimes are a good time for this. (In fact, family mealtimes in themselves are an important part of forming a team.) If you don't talk to them all at once, they will be individually motivated by being involved, but it won't do anything for their feeling of team unity.

Team briefing

The technique: In order to engender a strong and positive group identity within the team, you need to talk to them as a team. Hold regular team briefing sessions in which you pass on information which affects the group, and give them a chance to ask questions.

When anything important is happening in the family, call everyone together and brief them: "OK guys. We've got the builders in for the next fortnight, and here's what's going to be happening." Have a system – without making things incongruously formal – that they listen while you give the briefing, and then ask questions afterwards. If they're not happy and want a whinge, ask them to save it until after the briefing session. "I'm happy to talk to you about why you're not allowed to drive the mini-digger, but let's finish this first."

But you don't have to save the team briefing for major events. If you really want to inculcate a feeling of unity, the best system of all is a drip-feed approach. Keep topping up the team feeling with weekly sessions, even if they're only five minutes long. Again, mealtimes are an easy time to hold these sessions, and Sunday evening is a good time to outline the week ahead – but of course you should involve the kids in fixing a suitable time for a regular briefing session. The older they get, the harder it is to assemble all your kids at once. But don't make this an unpleasant issue. Just get them to agree a time that works for them all (of course, Catch 22, you may have to get them all together to agree such a time). Maybe Monday morning breakfast before school will do. It's not quite as relaxed as Sunday but if it works, go for it.

A team briefing at work should consist of imparting any information you need to in half a dozen key areas:

- People – anybody new or changed jobs, or been particularly successful
- Progress – how the team is doing against targets
- Policy – new procedures or policies, or old ones that need reiterating
- Problems – such as targets not being met, standards dropping, production problems
- Plans – future plans for the department or the organisation
- Action – current priorities

(That's according to The Work Foundation, and they should know.) You can make notes of anything you want to remember to say on any of these topics, and of course you won't necessarily have something to say under every heading every week. But let's just see how they apply to family rather than work life. Here are a few examples.

- People – This is a good opportunity for public praise, even if it's not news to anyone in the family. "Terrific exam results, Ellen, especially for Physics and History." Another entry for this category would be "We've got your cousin Paul coming to stay for a week on Thursday."
- Progress – You can update everyone on how the building works are going, and congratulate everyone for coping with

the upheaval. And you can tell them what their reward will be if they can get below the 10 minute barrier for clearing up after the meal.

- Policy – This is an opportunity to remind the family that if they don't bring back coffee mugs from their bedrooms every day, they won't be allowed to take drinks there. Also, although you generally give the briefing yourself while the children listen, you can occasionally ask them to fill the rest of the family in on some area they are responsible for: "Megan, you've got a new system for the video cupboard. Do you want to explain it to everyone?"
- Problems – Chores are being skipped, bedtimes are slipping, the car is so full of empty pizza boxes and chocolate bar wrappers that the family doesn't fit in it any more. These are collective problems – individual problems should be dealt with outside the team briefing.
- Plans – This is when you should have warned everyone a few weeks ago that you were going to get the builders in. It's also where you mention that you're going to need a new car (although this isn't the time to discuss it in detail – you can agree to do that later).
- Action – If you have practical information to act on, this is the time to impart it. For example: "Don't forget, we've had the new burglar alarm installed now. So the last person to go to bed each night needs to remember to set it." Or maybe, "Don't forget to take your lunch money for this term into school tomorrow morning."

Needless to say, you need to keep this fun for the kids. Don't get all formal and businesslike on them. They'll understand that the points you're making are serious. There shouldn't be any trouble here, either. If there are big problem areas you might refer to them here, but deal with them separately. For example, if cleaning out the rabbit hutch is leading to rows, under 'problems' you can simply say "We all know about the rabbit cleaning problem, but we'll talk about it some other time." That way, team briefings are never going to be unpleasant, so there's no reason for anyone to avoid them.

Team briefings for the family are important, but they don't have to take long. Sometimes they may last 10 minutes, some weeks it could be as little as three minutes. I'm sure your kids will let you know if it's going on too long. But they have a psychological function in bringing the team together, as well as a practical purpose, so do make sure you hold the meeting even if some things might have waited or could have been said to the children individually. You'll get more benefit doing it this way.

Deal with conflict and rivalry within the team

Some conflict is inevitable. In fact, it can even be a good thing. Healthy competition can drive people to even greater results, whether it's the number of sales each one notches up in a month, or whether it's who can swim a length of the pool fastest, or be the first to learn to ride a bicycle.

But you don't need telling that a lot of the conflicts that arise between children aren't a good thing however you look at them. If you follow all the guidelines in this book, you should find that your family life is as calm and pleasant as anyone's and far better than most. But of course there will still be the occasional row. At home, as at work, there are three main causes of conflict between people:

- One person feels they are being treated unfairly
- One person feels excluded from the team
- There is a straightforward personality clash

Let's take a look at how to deal with each of these in turn.

One person feels they are being treated unfairly

The technique: You need to establish the facts, and if the person is indeed being treated unfairly you should rectify this. However, even if you think things are fair, if someone *feels* they are being treated unfairly this will still lead to conflict. So get everyone involved together, and ask the person to express what they feel is unfair. Then you can oversee the discussion, making sure no one gets personal or heated, and help them to reach a solution.

In team terms, we're talking about children who feel that their siblings are doing less work or easier chores. If the gripe is only with you, it's not a team issue (and we'll have dealt with it in the last chapter). But if Eloise reckons that Mike only has 10 minutes of chores a day while she has 20, she may be giving Mike a hard time for not taking over some of hers.

If you're a team, you have to resolve these problems as a team and not individually. You need Mike there, even if Eloise is being unrealistic. Maybe she's just a slow worker, and if they swopped chores, she'd *still* have 20 minutes' worth to Mike's 10. But with Mike there too, the conflict can be discussed openly. Bear in mind that there are lots of reasons people can feel things are unfair. Maybe Eloise doesn't care how long the chores take, but she feels her tasks are less important, or less interesting.

If Mike can see she has a point, he is much more likely to co-operate in an atmosphere of open, friendly discussion. No one's blaming him or giving him a hard time, but he knows from experience that if he trades chores until Eloise is happy, he'll come in for plenty of praise. And if he insists her chores are no different from his, he won't mind changing, will he?

One person feels excluded from the team

The technique: If you want your team to pull together, you need to give them a sense of being a team. Once they learn that being part of a co-operative team is more pleasant than not, they will quickly learn to incorporate everyone into the team. You can help by treating everyone with equal importance – even though they may not have equal seniority. If you show that you listen to everyone's view equally, and give everyone responsibilities that suit their skills, they will all learn to treat each other the same way.

This problem arises most commonly in families when you have three children. Two play together, and the third is excluded because they're "too little" or "only a girl". Of course, you can't make your children play with each other all the time. And it's good for them to spend time alone or with friends outside the family. But if the exclusion is handled unkindly ("Shove off! We don't want you around"), you'll have an unpleasant conflict to deal with.

If you've been following the rules earlier in this chapter, you should find that this arises much less often. Once your children feel like a team they will be much more inclined to do things together. And when they don't want to, they'll say so nicely.

But you can help things along, too, by setting an example. If you allow the children to join in with you – fixing the car, decorating the spare bedroom, assembling the flat-packed wardrobe – they are more likely to allow each other to join in with them. And if you show by example that everyone is capable of handling responsibility and can be trusted to behave sensibly, again you'll find your children follow suit with each other. So you'll still get the occasional complaint of "He won't let me play with his leeches!", but you'll encounter far fewer conflicts arising from a sense of exclusion.

There is a personality clash

The technique: Bring the two people involved together, and get them to talk to each other directly, using feedback techniques. Point out to them that it is important to compromise: it's worth it to prevent the conflict. And encourage them to see the problem from the other person's perspective – it often makes it easier for people to compromise once they realise how the other person feels.

You cannot resolve a personality clash by acting as a go-between. You must bring the two children involved together to discuss it. It is their problem, and they must learn to resolve their own problems, not rely on you to sort it out for them. In any case, if you deal with them separately, they will each wonder what was said about the problem when they weren't there.

Most personality based conflict between brothers and sisters revolves around the same few characteristics. For example, there are frequent blow-ups because one of your children is always slow and late for everything, while the other does things in a rush and hates hanging around waiting for their brother or sister. Resolving this one, single problem could remove a sizeable proportion of the conflicts. So get to the root cause and deal with that, rather than tackle each incident individually.

The time to arrange this session is not when they are busy bawling each other out, but later on when they are getting on fine again and in a co-operative mood. You need to mediate, but get them to use feedback techniques:

- Allow the other one to finish what they are saying.
- Focus on the problem and not the other one's personality ("I get frustrated hanging around", not "You're always late for everything").

- Talk about their own feelings, not the other one's actions ("I feel stressed when I'm being rushed").

Before you start the session, get them both to recognise that life would be pleasanter for everyone if this conflict were resolved. Then explain that this can only happen if they are both prepared to make some concessions. Make it clear that if they can't be adult about this and agree a compromise between them, you will impose one. But you would far rather they sorted it out for themselves.

Your role is to keep out of the discussion except to remind them of the feedback rules if they start to stray from them. And, since you are only a referee, you must not express any personal view. You might personally agree that Jack is unreasonably slow at getting ready for almost anything, but it won't help if you say so. And even if he is, Ned has still got to learn to cope with it without losing his rag. So don't show any bias. You'll also need to make sure that both of them are making a compromise, rather than one of them making all the concessions in order to keep things sweet.

Don't let them leave the discussion until they have agreed a solution. Maybe Jack should be allowed to set the departure time when they go out (within reason), on condition that he then sticks to it. Ned may not get to leave as quickly as he'd like, but instead of hanging around he can simply delay getting ready until two minutes before Jack's stipulated time. You may be able to help, too, by agreeing to give them both plenty of notice when you all need to go out as a family. No sudden announcements of "We're off shopping. Everyone ready?"

Once they've made their agreement, let them know that if the conflict and problems continue, you'll have to get them to sit down again and find a better solution – or accept one of yours.

And finally, when they have made a decision on how to resolve the conflict, don't forget to praise them for having addressed the problem in such an adult way (and don't let on that half the adults you've met at work couldn't have done it).

Summary

One of the great things about employing team building skills with your children is that the rewards keep growing. The more they feel like part of a team, the more they will want to co-operate with each other, and the fewer rows they will have. So you're doing them a big favour in helping them to strengthen their relationships, but you're doing yourself a big favour too in making family life more enjoyable.

Conclusion

All the techniques in this book have a proven track record in the workplace, helping to build more successful and happier organisations. And you'll find that they have the same effect at home, building more successful and happier families. And what more could you honestly ask (except to have that damn rabbit hutch cleaned out)?

Once you realise how many skills you have already learned at work that you can apply at home, you'll find that it becomes natural to use them with your children. To begin with, you may wonder which skills to use when but, if you think about it, this isn't a worry at work. There, you barely think about most of these skills at all: they're instinctive. You don't remind yourself to smile every time a customer appears. You're barely even aware that you're doing it.

Building up the same portfolio of skills at home is a very similar process. You'll have found, reading this book, that some of the points really ring true, while others don't seem to apply to you at the moment. For example, if you have only one child the team building skills won't be relevant.

So practise the skills that are important to you at the moment. If you have a child who complains about the slightest thing ("I asked for my cocoa slightly hot, and you've given it to me very warm!"), master the techniques for dealing with complaints. With a child like this, it won't be long before these skills become second nature (believe me – I've been there).

If you have a second child, you'll find that after a couple of years you'll want to practise team building in the family. (Maybe around the time your older child starts yelling, "I don't want a little brother. I hate him, and I wish he'd never been born!") You'll soon learn to incorporate team building techniques into your repertoire and you'll practise them so instinctively that you won't even know you're doing it.

When your daughter hits the really mischievous stage, you'll learn about how to use discipline skills. When it gets really tough to elicit any kind of agreement from your teenager, you'll master negotiating skills (actually, you're doing well if you can get as far as the teenage years before you have to learn these). When your toddler interrupts constantly and then throws a tantrum if you don't respond instantly, you'll want to reread the section on customer relations techniques and incorporate them into your parenting style.

Each time you encounter a behavioural problem that shows signs of becoming a habit, that's when you need to raid your business skills for another technique or two to add to your toolkit. Before long, you'll find that you're as skilled at parenting as you are in business. I'm afraid you won't get a promotion for your pains. But you will get an easier life, more fun, and at the end of the process you'll have produced a terrific adult or two whose company you'll really enjoy. And if you play your cards right, they'll have all the skills they need to leave home successfully and give you some peace at last.

$$e = mc^2$$